*The*

# MARTHA BECK

## COLLECTION

*Expecting Adam*

*Finding Your Own North Star*

*The Joy Diet*

*Leaving the Saints*

*The 4-Day Win*

*Steering by Starlight*

*Finding Your Way in a Wild New World*

# The
# **MARTHA BECK**
# COLLECTION

*Essays for Creating
Your Right Life*

**VOLUME ONE**

Published by Martha Beck, Inc.
For further information, contact:

MARTHA BECK, INC.
3940-7 Broad Street #405,
San Luis Obispo, CA 93401
www.marthabeck.com

ISBN: 978-0-9893067-0-6
Library of Congress Control Number:  2013937882
Printed in the United States

Book and cover design by Laura Shaw Design, www.lshawdesign.com

........................................................

*To my wonderful tribe of coaches.*
*May you thrive forever, and may we*
*share many adventures on our quest*
*to heal whatever little part of the*
*world we can. I love you all.*

........................................................

# CONTENTS

# FOREWORD

Every now and again, some kind stranger will come up to me at the supermarket or opium den or wherever, and say something like: "I really enjoy your articles in the *Oprah Magazine*. I've gotten a lot from them."

I always try to respond graciously, with a smile that's honestly happy and gratitude that's certainly genuine. But inside, I'm thinking, "What? You like my columns? Why? What useful thing on God's green earth could you possibly derive from these little riffs of prose that fall so far short of my hopes for them?"

It's even worse when people want to ask me about specific columns, because I rarely remember the content. When I try to remember a certain column, I just recall the blue glow of my computer screen, dimly lighting a house where my loved ones were fast asleep. I recall wearily rubbing my eyes, my hair, my forehead, trying desperately to put vague ideas into linear thoughts that make some sort of sense.

This first-draft process usually takes all night, at which point I have a fairly cogent piece approximately four times as long as my allotted 1600 words. I spend about three days cutting away the deadwood, and at the end I have a lean little piece of what looks like drivel to me. I email this to my editor, who makes a few excellent suggestions. Then I simply move on and never think about that column again—that is, until a kind stranger approaches.

At those times, I remember an Indigo Girls song about Virginia Woolf. The lyrics mention that Woolf's writing is "a kind of a telephone line through time, and the voice at the other end comes as a long lost friend. So I know I'm all right." Those nights, when I think I'm alone, I'm really placing a call through time, to the person who will read my words. And the listener at the other end of that line already feels like a long-lost friend. That's how I can make my shy, perfectionistic self keep writing. That, and horse tranquilizers.

Seriously, it always feels like a terrible gamble to put your heart on a page and throw it out into the world. Without the support of my family, my friends, my wonderful coaches, my editors, and all the other glorious beings in my life, I simply could not do it. And without those kind comments from people who managed to find something useful in my words, I could not continue it.

One of my editors recently asked what kind of self-help books I'm reading recently. I realized I no longer read self-help literature. When I mentioned this to my daughter

Lizzy, she said, "Well, Mom, you self-helped." And perhaps that's the reason people find something heartening in my writing. I only put down on paper what works for me, and since I started out as a human train wreck, the ways I've learned to be happy also work for others.

If you are one of those others, thank you so very much for your interest in reading this compilation of some favorite columns I've written during my long stint in the magazine business. And remember that the finger that points to the moon is not the moon. Anything thoughtful or amusing or true you find on any page is mirroring your essence—that's how you recognize it.

So these words started out as mine, but as you read them, the ones you feel are true become yours. Please jettison anything that doesn't resonate for you. Keep the good stuff, and know that I am inexpressibly grateful to you for picking up all the telephone calls I've placed in the middle of the night for such a long time. And if you accost me in public, know that the blankness in my eyes is pure astonishment that you found meaning in yourself because of something I wrote.

*Hello, this is Martha, writing a foreword for her compilation book in the middle of the night in January 2013. Do you have a few minutes? Is this a good time? Well, then, let's talk.*

—MARTHA BECK

# How to Know It's Real Love

*Is it love, or a mutual strangulation society?*
*Here are five ways to get a real grip on the real thing.*

•

I n a folktale that has been retold for centuries in many variations (one of which is Shakespeare's *King Lear*), an elderly king asks his three daughters how much they love him. The two older sisters deliver flowery speeches of filial adoration, but the youngest says only "I love you as meat loves salt." The king, insulted by this homely simile, banishes the youngest daughter and divides his kingdom between the older two, who promptly kick him out on his royal heinie. He seeks refuge in the very house where his third daughter is working as a scullery maid. Recognizing her father, the daughter asks the cook to prepare his meal without salt. The king eats a few tasteless mouthfuls, and then bursts into tears. "All along," he cries, "It was my youngest daughter who really loved me!" The daughter reveals herself and all ends happily (except in *King Lear,* where pretty much everybody dies).

This story survived throughout Europe for a very long time because it is highly instructive: It reminds listeners that in matters of love, choosing style over substance is disastrous. It also helps us know when we're making that mistake. Salt is unique in that its taste doesn't cover up the food it seasons but enhances whatever flavor was there to begin with. Real love, real commitment, does the same thing.

Each of the following five statements is the polar opposite of what most Americans see as loving commitment. But these are "meat loves salt" commitments, as necessary as they are unconventional. Only if you and your beloved can honestly say them to each other is your relationship likely to thrive.

## One
### "I can live without you, no problem."

"I can't live," wails the singer, "if living is without you." It sounds so tragically deep to say that losing your lover's affections would make life unlivable—but have you ever been in a relationship with someone whose survival truly seemed to depend on your love? Someone who sat around waiting for you to make life bearable, who threatened to commit suicide if you ever broke up? Or have you found yourself on the grasping side of the equation, needing your partner the way you need oxygen? The emotion that fuels this kind of relationship isn't love; it's desperation. It can feel romantic at first, but over time it invariably fails to meet either partner's needs.

The statement "I can't survive without you" reflects not adult attraction but infancy, a phase when we really would have died if our caretakers hadn't stayed close by, continuously anticipating our needs. The hunger for total nurturing usually means we're in the middle of a psychological regression, feeling like abandoned infants who need parenting now, now, now! If this is how you feel, don't start dating. Start therapy. Counseling can teach you how to get your needs met by the only person responsible for them: you. The "I can't live without you" syndrome ends when we learn to care for ourselves as tenderly and attentively as a good mother. At that point, we're ready to form stable, lasting attachments that can last a lifetime. "I can live without you" is an assurance that sets the stage for real love.

## Two
### "My love for you will definitely change."

Most human beings seem innately averse to change. Once we've established some measure of comfort or stability, we want to nail it in place so that there's no possibility of loss. It's understandable, then, that the promise "My love for you will never change" is a hot seller. Unfortunately, this is another promise that is more likely to scuttle a relationship than shore it up.

The reason is that everything—and everyone—is constantly changing. We age, grow, learn, get sick, get well, gain weight, lose weight, find new interests, and drop old ones. And when two individuals are constantly in flux, their relationship must be fluid to survive. Many people fear that if their love is free to change, it will vanish. The opposite is true. A love that is allowed to adapt to new circumstances is virtually indestructible. Infatuation relaxes into calm companionship, then flares again as we see new things to love about each other. In times of trouble and illness, obligation may feel stronger than attraction—until one day we realize that hanging in there through troubled times has bonded us more deeply than ever before. Like running water, changing love finds its way past obstacles. Freezing it in place makes it fragile, rigid, and all too likely to shatter.

### Three
### "You're not everything I need."

I'm a big fan of sexual monogamy, but I'm puzzled by lovers who claim that their romantic partner is the only person they need in their lives or that time together is the only activity necessary for emotional fulfillment. Humans are designed to live in groups, explore ideas, and constantly learn new skills. Trying to get all this input from one person is like trying to get a full range of vitamins by eating only ice cream. When a couple believes "We must fulfill all of each other's needs," each becomes exhausted by the effort to be all things to the other and neither can develop fully as an individual.

It amazes me how often my clients' significant others feel threatened when the clients revive childhood passions or take up new hobbies. I encourage people to bring their spooked spouses to a session so we can discuss their fears. The hurt partners usually come in sounding something like this: "How come you have to spend three hours a week playing tennis (or gardening or painting)? Are you saying I'm not enough to keep you happy?" The healthiest response to such questions is "That's right, our relationship isn't enough to make me completely happy—and if I pretended it were, I'd stunt my soul and poison my love for you. Ever thought about what you'd like to do on your own?" Sacrificing all our individual needs doesn't strengthen a relationship. Mutually supporting each other's personal growth does.

## Four
### "I won't always hold you close."

There's a thin line between a romantic statement like "I love you so much, I want to share my life with you until death do us part" and the lunatic-fringe anthem "I love you so much that if you try to leave me, I'll kill you." People who say such things love others the way spiders love flies; they love to capture them, wrap them in immobilizing fetters, and drain nourishment out of them at peckish moments. This is not the kind of love you want.

The way you can tell real love from spider love is simple: Possessiveness and exploitation involve controlling the loved one, whereas true love is based on setting the beloved free to make his or her own choices. How you use the word *make* is also a tip-off. When you hear yourself saying "He makes me feel X" or "He made me do Y," you're playing the victimized, trussed-up fly. Even more telling are sentences like "I've got to make him see that he's wrong" or "I'll hide what I really think because it would make him angry." You are not the victim but the crafty spider, withholding and using manipulation to control your mate's feelings and actions. Either strategy means that someone is being held too close, wrapped in spider silk.

Getting out of this sticky situation is simple: Tell the truth, the whole truth, and nothing but the truth. Begin by taking responsibility for your own choices—including the choice to obey the spider man who may have you in his thrall. Then communicate your real feelings, needs, and desires to your partner, without trying to force the reaction you want. If your relationship can't thrive in the clear light of honesty, it is better to get out of it than to sink further into manipulation and control.

## Five
### "You and I aren't one."

Perhaps you are neither a spider nor a fly but a chameleon that morphs to match the one you love. Or you may date

chameleons, choosing partners who conform to your personality. Either way, you're not in a healthy relationship. In
fact, you're not in a relationship at all.

I used to tune in so acutely to my loved ones' wants
and needs that I literally didn't know my own. This denial
of self ultimately turned into resentment, poisoning several
close relationships. Then—once burned, twice shy—I went
briefly to the opposite extreme. I found myself having a lot
of lackluster lunches with folks who hung on my every word
and agreed with everything I said. Narcissistic I may be, but
Narcissus I'm not; hanging out with a human looking glass,
no matter how flattering, left me lonely.

If you're living by the "We are one" ideal, it's high time
you found out how terrific love for two can be. Follow your
heart in a direction your partner wouldn't go. Dare to explore
your differences. Agree to disagree. If you're accustomed to
disappearing, this will allow you to see that you can be loved
as you really are. If you tend to dominate, you'll find out
how interesting it is to love an actual person rather than a
human mirror.

Buddha once said that just as we can know the ocean
because it always tastes of salt, we can recognize enlightenment because it always tastes of freedom. There's no essential difference between real love and enlightenment. While
many people see commitment as a trap, its healthy versions

actually free both lovers, bring out the flavor of their true selves, and build a love that is satisfying, lasting, and altogether delicious.

FEBRUARY 2002

# Ready...Aim...Oh, Well
## Why You Need to Embrace Imperfection

*I'm human. Humans goof. So why do I get my knickers in a twist about being flawless 24/7? As a reformed perfectionist, learn how I silenced the barking mosquito in my head.*

a t the moment (though not, I hope, by the time you read it), this article is a mess of redundant, poorly phrased, haphazardly punctuated drivel. At the top, written in bold capital letters, is the working title I use for all new projects: shitty first draft. I owe this graceful phrase to writer-teacher Anne Lamott, who recommends the shitty first draft as an indispensable phase of literary creation— and, for that matter, any other human endeavor. A New Age-y friend of mine was once horrified to see my production title. "You manifest what you project," he cautioned. "If you want your writing to be perfect, you have to think of it as perfect." Maybe that works for him. Not me. I've never written anything within shrieking distance of perfect. Even trying scares me so much that the first time I did it, when I was assigned to write a poem for a middle school assignment, my doctor—my pediatrician, mind you—had to put me on Valium.

Most people realize that perfectionism, as Lamott puts it in her book *Bird by Bird*, "is the voice of the oppressor, the enemy of the people. It will keep you cramped and insane your whole life." But seriously unwell people such as me run into trouble when we try to let go of perfectionism. We end up getting perfectionistic about our attempts to stop being perfectionists. I began finding my way out of this psychological morass when I heard the Buddhist saying "To be enlightened is to be without anxiety over imperfection." Years after adopting this perspective, I'm still a perfectionist, but here's the thing: I don't care.

I've found some reliable ways to reduce my anxiety about my imperfections, including my imperfection at ridding myself of perfectionism. I encourage you to try doing the following exercises—imperfectly.

### Exercise One
## **Personify Your Inner Perfectionist**

I've been using the term *perfectionist* as though it's something you can be. Actually, I think it's something people have, like brain damage. Separating your innate personality from your perfectionism frees you to confront it, rather than get lost in it. To that end, I recommend giving your perfectionism its own name and face.

Can't picture this inner critic? Start by thinking about a mistake you've made recently. Let the voice of the oppressor berate you ("You dumb, clumsy, fat, boring..." etc.). Listen: Does that voice sound familiar? Does it belong to your wicked stepmother, your boss, your ex-spouse, an amalgam of your least-favorite movie critics? Try to summon a visual image of the tyrant. Scribble a picture of it, and do something insulting to this picture whenever your perfectionist acts up. In time, as you neutralize the destructive power inherent in this aspect of yourself, you may well lose all fear of it. By just externalizing and rejecting your inner critic, you can decrease your anxiety considerably.

### Exercise Two
**Embrace Creative Hopelessness**

Your perfectionism will tell you that it is your ticket to perfection, your one chance at a flawless existence. This may be true for you. If your brand of perfectionism has created a life free of mistakes or shortcomings, by all means, carry on. But if you're anything like me, perfectionism usually paralyzes you before you begin, stiffens you until you screw up, and sends shame howling through your consciousness even if you do well. It's time to wake up and smell this dark-roasted little truth: Perfectionism never delivers on its promise of perfection. It does not work.

Some psychologists use the phrase "creative hopelessness" to describe the moments when we realize that our psychological strategies are useless or counterproductive. Embracing this hopelessness—in this case, relinquishing the delusional hope that we can or must be flawless—allows us to seek happiness in the only place it can be found: our real, messy, imperfect experience. To arrive at creative hopelessness, write down your reason for maintaining your perfectionism. It'll probably be something like this:

---

### PERFECTIONIST CREDO

*If I try hard enough and*
*I'm very careful and*
*I follow all the rules,*
*everything will go right and*
*everyone will love me and*
*I'll feel good all the time.*

---

Now ask yourself the following question, made famous by our good friend Dr. Phil: So, how's it working for you?

The most common response I get when I ask this question, whether I'm addressing myself or a client, is laughter. Releasing our doomed, anxious hope for perfection opens us to the joy available in our actual lives—especially if we move on to the next exercise.

### Exercise Three
## Do Something Badly

Gradual, safe exposure to whatever makes us anxious is always the most powerful way of eliminating anxiety. In order not to be cowed by imperfection, you must not only accept the imperfect, but also seek it. Take shitty first drafts—please. I never sit down to write an excellent first draft, or even a good one. My goal is always to create something readers wouldn't even want to scrape off their shoes. Adopting this objective gives me permission to do the lousy job I'm sure to do on any initial attempt. It gets me through the excruciating process of going from Nothing to Something: no matter how odious it may be, turning it into Something Better is usually less work, and you may even turn it into Something Good. The first step toward achieving excellence is imperfection.

Try this: Choose something you've always wanted to do—paint, jog, whatever. Now set out to do this thing *really* badly. Your inner perfectionist may erupt in violent protest. Thank her for sharing, then reward yourself for daring to do a terrible job. An even better option is the buddy system: Commit with a friend that you'll both do something really terribly, then praise each other for following through.

If you have the guts to do this, you'll find that contrary to conventional wisdom, people love you when you're openly imperfect. I discovered this when teaching business school, a task I approached with little preparation, less talent, and all the confidence of a snowball headed for hell. On my desk, I kept a box labeled "Criticisms and Recommendations," in which my students could deposit anonymous suggestions about how I might improve my teaching. I learned so much from the students that my teaching improved rapidly. This is what happens whenever we free ourselves to grow by letting ourselves do something badly.

Exercise Four
## Just Keep Showing Up

"Ninety percent of staying in shape," says one of my professional-athlete clients, "is getting to the gym." I've heard high-achieving people say the same thing about pretty much every human enterprise: Successful musicians just show up, day after day, to practice their instruments. Successful businessmen show up for their customers. Successful writers show up at the blank page. Ask any of them and they'll tell you that most days, they come nowhere near perfection. What makes them winners is not instant excellence but the sheer dumb repetition of showing up.

The same is true of the even more significant task of sustaining human relationships. Consider the people who have most blessed your life—are they the folks you remember as perfect or those who were simply, consistently there for you? You don't have to be perfect for your friends, your children, or your beloved; you just have to show up.

You may have noticed that this article, though edited since its initial shitty-first-draft incarnation, is still far from perfect. Do I wish this were not the case? You bet your ass I do. My inner perfectionist (an immaculately dressed social-ite who carries an arrest warrant, a flamethrower, and a bad case of rabies) is outraged by my literary shortcomings. But I have learned to let her fuss without succumbing to the anxiety she encourages. Long experience as a profoundly flawed person has taught me this unexpected truth: that welcoming imperfection is the way to accomplish what perfectionism promises but never delivers. It gives us our best performance, and genuine acceptance in the family of human—and by that I mean imperfect—beings.

JULY 2003

# Why Are People Mean?

*Someone insults you (and your little dog, too).*
*You can retaliate, whimper—or exercise your own vast*
*power. Here's how to rewrite your own character.*

The first time I saw a T-shirt that said "mean people suck," I thought, Now, there is a heartfelt sentiment, succinctly expressed. I only wished I'd been the author. I mention this because recently I've encountered several mean people, and I've had to remind myself that the concept of authorship is key to surviving these experiences.

I don't know about you, but my favorite ways of reacting to mean people are (1) getting mean right back or (2) lying down quietly to display the word *welcome!* written where my spine used to be. Annoyingly, my job constantly reminds me that there's a more responsible and effective way to live. That's how it is for us authors. I say "us" because you're an author, too. Not all of us write for publication, but every living person has the power of authorship when it comes to composing our lives. Meanness emerges when we believe that we have no such power, that we're passive receptors of life's vagaries. Inner peace follows when we begin responding to cruelty—our own and other people's—with the authority we've possessed all along.

Why are people mean? Here's the short answer: They're hurt. Here's the long answer: They're really hurt. At some point, somebody—their parents, their lovers, Lady Luck—did them dirty. They were crushed. And they're still afraid the pain will never stop, or that it will happen again.

There. I've just described every single person living on planet Earth.

The fact is that we've all been hurt, and we're all wounded, but not all of us are mean. Why not? Because some people realize that their history of suffering can be a hero's saga rather than a victim's whine, depending on how they "write" it. The moment we begin tolerating meanness, in ourselves or others, we are using our authorial power in the service of wrongdoing. We have both the capacity and the obligation to do better.

"You know," I once said to my 7-year-old daughter, "when I was your age, I wanted to go to Sherwood Forest and meet Robin Hood." She looked at me with alarm, then cautiously asked, "Mom, do you know what fiction means?" In retrospect, I have to admit the true answer to this question was no. Sure, I realized that Robin Hood was a fictional character. But I wasn't yet aware how much of my worldview was fiction, how powerfully I was shaping the characters and plot of my own life story.

We perceive events as story lines. We continually (though often unconsciously) tell ourselves tales about life, and since no story can include every tiny event, we edit and spin the facts into the stories we prefer. Many of our stories are pure fabrication, and all of them are biased, dominated by our flair for the dramatic, our theories about life, and our fears. A typical mean person's story line goes like this: "I am a victim; people want to hurt me; I must hurt them first to be safe." This is why mean people may turn ugly when you say something like "Please pass the salt" or "Hey, it's raining." They immediately rewrite whatever they hear to support their story line ("She's saying I'm a bad cook" or "He's bringing up the weather to avoid talking about us"). The story, not other people's behavior, both motivates and excuses their hostility.

If we react to this type of meanness with cruelty of our own, we climb onto the wheel of suffering that drives all conflict, from lovers' spats to wars: You're mean to me so I'm mean to you so you're meaner to me so I'm meaner to you....

We'll stay on this sickening merry-go-round until we decide to get off—and please note that I did not say "when others stop being mean to us." We can ride the wheel of suffering when no one else is even present (telling ourselves the same old sad story again and again), and we can leave it even in the midst of violent persecution. The way out is not found in changing our circumstances but in the power of authorship.

Like any work of fiction, your life story begins with description. Try sitting down and writing a one-page account of your life (no stressing over style; this is for your eyes only).

Now go get a hat. That's right, a hat. When you wear this hat, you become the Reader, a different person from the Author. Put on your hat and read what you've written, pretending you've never seen it. Ask yourself: Is this the story of a hero or a victim? Is it a tale of the terrible things that have happened to the central character (you), or does it speak in terms of the choices you've made to create those circumstances? Do you dwell on vengeance or gratitude? Do difficult people and situations appear as forces that control you or as problems you are busily solving?

Now take off your hat and get a second piece of paper. Write another description of your life, one that is more heroic than the last (if your first story was valiant, make this one even more so). Mention times you chose wisely, instances when people were kind to you, moments you knew that no matter how bad things looked, you were going to succeed.

Don your hat, read your new history, and see how it compares to the first draft. I suspect that you'll find it much more interesting and enjoyable. You've just exercised the storytelling talent that will take you off the wheel of suffering: the power to write your character as a hero rather than a victim.

This skill not only keeps you from being mean to others—if you're consciously composing your life as a hero's saga, you won't excuse your own cruelty or anyone else's—but also guides you to healthy options when others are mean to you. You'll respond bravely but compassionately to the villains you encounter. You may need practice, but you can compose your hero's saga with your actions, not just the written word. Feel hemmed in by obligations to children, siblings, parents? You are free to say no, even if it rocks the family boat. Trapped in an unenlightened culture? You are free to act on your own principles, whatever the response. Take your liberty. Use your power. Rewrite every memory of your own victimization as a hero's adventure.

One definition of the word mean is "small." Mean people live small, think small, and feel small—the smaller, the meaner. For example, after boxer Mike Tyson bit off part of an opponent's ear, his comment was "What am I supposed to do? I've got children to raise." This made no sense, since Tyson was paid nearly $30 million after losing that fight. A likely psychological explanation is that when he was physically overwhelmed, he felt like a child himself. He bit like a playground runt to protect the defenseless little person he thought himself to be.

The belief that we are smaller and less powerful than others underlies most meanness, even when that belief is delusional. But we can also use our author's imagination to size things in our favor. Think of a person who's been nasty to you. Imagine that person shrinking to one inch tall.

Picture your enemy stomping around in the palm of your hand, yelling or sneering all the customary cruelties. You'll find that if your critic is making a valid point, it will still sound accurate, but mere verbal abuse is hilarious when squeaked in the voice of an inch-tall Mini-Mean.

Whatever your reaction to this tiny villain, that's probably the best way to react to your life-size challenger. If the insults are laughable, just laugh. If the mean person has a point, tell her that you get it, but she could stand to work on her people skills. Practice what you would say if you felt big and invulnerable, then say it, even if you're scared. Be "big" by responding to cruelty with honest calm rather than aggression or submissiveness.

Ernest Hemingway claimed the most essential talent for a good writer was simply a "built-in, shockproof shit detector." Great authorship is all about truth. To write the stories of our lives as honestly as possible, we must thoroughly reject crap. This is especially useful when cruelty masquerades as kindness. Some of the most merciless behavior ever perpetrated looks very nice. The sweeter a lie sounds, the meaner it really is.

"Honey, people are whispering about your weight." "Stop talking back, or you'll lose that husband of yours." "Oh, sweetheart, that's way too big a dream for you." Statements like these may be well-intentioned feedback—or spite. The difference is that honesty, even the tough stuff, makes you feel clearer and stronger, while meanness leaves you mired in shame, despair, and frailty.

This is true physically as well as psychologically. I sometimes make my clients do push-ups while repeating feedback they've been given, such as "I need to lose 20 pounds" or "I should be nicer." If the statement is false, the strength literally drains from their bodies. If it's true, they become stronger. One client, a couch potato in her 60s, started cranking out literally hundreds of push-ups once she rejected the feedback she was getting from her husband and chose to believe what her heart was telling her. Try this yourself to see what your internal detection system reveals about the feedback you've received. Trust, remember, and revisit honest advice. Muck everything else right out of your mind.

If you opt to write your life consciously, you'll find that a tale acknowledging your hero's strength feels truer than one depicting you as a victim. You'll see that whatever your physical size, you really are a bigger person than any bully. You'll learn that the truth, no matter how hard, always strengthens you more than a lie, no matter how nice. On the other hand, if you don't take up your authority, you give mean people the power to write your life for you. In the end, they will make you one of them. That should give you the motivation you need to take up your authority, because let's face it: Mean people suck.

NOVEMBER 2003

# The Halo Effect
## Are You Too Good for Your Own Good?

*Are you the kind of person who thinks she's being good (self-sacrificing! angelic!) by cooing over things you hate and sucking up to strangers for tiny morsels of approval? I have been there and back and encourage you to hang up your wings.*

always wait until the house is empty before I practice the piano. I love playing, but I don't do it well, and I'm embarrassed to bother others with my discordant fumbling. One day not long ago, I sent my children off to school and began plunking away in happy solitude—until I decided to play a certain Bach *cantata*. This piece seems to be a favorite of my beagle, Cookie. Whenever I play it, he hurries into the room and lies down under the piano, ears perked. Sure enough, after a few bars I heard paw steps in the hallway. Cookie appeared, plopped down near the pedals, and half closed his eyes, listening. I couldn't have been more flattered by a standing ovation at Carnegie Hall.

Then, disaster. I missed a note. For a moment I thought I could recover, but the error had a domino effect, and I started messing up all over the place. My fingers began to shake. I stopped breathing and started sweating, horrified that I was ruining Cookie's listening pleasure. In case you're not already marveling at the depth of my mental illness, let me reprise that for you: I was reduced to a nervous wreck because I couldn't play the piano correctly for my dog.

It was one of those moments when the cheesecloth of denial rips right through and you're left staring at the ugly truth. That day I finally admitted what I had become: I was not just a nice lady. Not just a people pleaser. I was an approval whore.

## Causes and Consequences of Approval Prostitution

We approval whores are people who will do anything to get affirmation and acceptance from others. We're similar to crack whores, only more dysfunctional. At least drug-addicted prostitutes know they're not being virtuous when they sell themselves to get high. Approval whores like me, on the other hand, tend to think that we're being good (saintly! angelic!) when we let others have their way with us in exchange for a hit of praise. The people in our lives are likely to reinforce our sickness, because we'll do pretty much anything to please them, and what's not to love about that?

Here's what: Being dependent on approval—so dependent that we barter away all our time, energy, and personal preferences to get it—ruins lives. It divorces us from our true selves, precludes real intimacy, and turns us into seething cesspools of suppressed rage (of course, I mean that in a nice way).

This is a good time of year to see what I'm talking about, because during the holidays even the most upstanding citizens are pressured to act a little slutty, approval-wise. You know the story: You coo in false delight while gnawing Aunt Wanda's petrified fruitcake or simulate ecstasy over a hand-knitted sweater that makes you look like an Amish land whale. Don't be ashamed; a little social prostitution during the holidays is virtually universal. However, if you are an approval whore year-round, this season may deepen your dysfunction to the point where your efforts to please become truly exhausting and other people's appreciation is less and less rewarding. If you feel drained or angry as the season progresses, it's time to get off the street. Learn to respect yourself. Give yourself the gift of the real you, clean and sober.

Pleasing others is like sex: When we do it because we really want to, it's a wonderfully life-affirming way to strengthen a relationship, but when it's motivated by obligation, powerlessness, or calculated advantage, it's the very definition of degrading. The key to an authentic emotional life, like the key to an authentic sex life, is to follow your real desires.

Suppose that every morning of this holiday season, you asked yourself what you really, truly wanted to do that day, and then did just that. Would you spend time you don't have buying things you can't afford for people you don't like? I didn't think so. Would you bake goodies, decorate, light the menorah or the Kwanzaa candles? Maybe. Would you engage in activities you love, in the places you love, with the people you love? Oh, yeah. That would be terrific!

So do it.

If this suggestion shocks you, if you're thinking, "Oh, I couldn't possibly," I regret to say you're on the trampy side. You've been selling out your passions to fit someone else's model of celebration. You probably think this is virtuous. I beg to differ. Acts of love done in the absence of love are obscene. This holiday eliminate them from your life. Learn to tolerate the anxiety of allowing people to disapprove of you.

Even I, one of the most hardened approval whores on earth, can do this. For example, when I lived in Southeast Asia, I was told that modest women always keep their heads down and their eyes on the ground. Here's what I saw during my first weeks in the exotic Far East: dirt, dirt, dirt, a snail(!), and dirt. I began to feel strangely shrunken, somehow less than a person who could look at the sky.

Finally, I decided to hold up my head no matter what the locals thought of me. Many Asians really were appalled. Women glared at me; men waggled their eyebrows (and occasionally other body parts). It was unnerving, but not as unnerving as assuming a posture that made me feel literally low. I vastly preferred being high on something more nourishing than approval: doing what felt right to me. I didn't lose my compulsion to seek social validation—like any addict, I'll always want my drug—but I learned to keep this desire from overwhelming me. Here are some strategies I've found helpful.

One

**Clarify your own morality.**

In our world of commingled cultures and traditions, we may confront innumerable moral codes, all different from one another. There is simply no way to gain approval from each of these disparate sources; trying to do so will make you feel even worse. Instead, clearly define your own moral code and then stick to it whether or not others approve. Right now think of something you plan to do during this holiday that you don't want to do: host a boorish guest, send greeting cards to folks you barely know, overspend to the point of serious financial strain. Then pretend that your best friend, rather than you, is the one contemplating this action. What would you say is her moral obligation? Don't think manners; think ethics. Would it be truly immoral for your friend to invite only guests she likes, or send no greeting cards, or buy fewer presents? Take some time figuring out your real beliefs.

If you decide your unpleasant plans aren't moral requirements, but you do them anyway, you're pimping yourself out. Anything we do solely to please others, in the absence of either real desire or moral necessity, is a way of selling ourselves, our lives, our energy. Ask yourself whether the dose of approval you expect to gain from this behavior is worth losing a piece of the real you. I'd be the last one to judge you if the answer is yes. All I ask is that you be aware that this is prostitution, not virtue.

## Two
### Get approval for getting disapproval.

One of the best ways to break your dependency on approval is to set up a situation in which the only way to get approval is to get disapproval. When I taught college-level sociology, I used to assign students to choose a social norm they thought was wrong or just plain silly, then deliberately violate it. The more disapproval they got, the higher their grade.

Once they were pursuing my approval (not to mention that of 90 classmates), some of my most people-pleasing students became embodiments of civil disobedience. One coed brought a homeless woman to lunch at her sorority house. A popular football player wore his grandfather's lederhosen to a nightclub. Another student went to church with "Resist religious intolerance" written on each forearm in magic marker. They all succeeded in garnering high levels of disapproval, which meant high levels of approval in my class. The realization that they could tolerate social censure was a major liberation; suddenly, these students felt free to be true to themselves, even when others condemned their actions.

To use this strategy, call a friend, tell her you're going out to get some disapproval, and ask her to lavish you with praise afterward. It works even better if you have several people—your best buddies, your therapy group, your sewing circle—waiting to hear the tale of your rebellion. The genius of the technique is that whether or not you carry through with your intentions, someone is going to disapprove. Learning to deal with that could prevent a lifetime of selling out.

### Three
## Agree to disagree.

When approval whores disagree with others, we react by not reacting. Instead of voicing our real position, we smile, nod, make cheerful mumbling sounds. As a result, everyone from the John Birch Society to the Hells Angels may think we agree with them. Some of us fear that if we begin voicing disagreement, we'll lose our friends and family. If this is true for you—if these people accept you only because you agree with everything they say—they're not friends or family, they're just customers from whom you regularly obtain your favorite drug. This is a thoroughly unhealthy situation.

Next time someone voices an opinion that contradicts your own, don't play dumb. Voice your thoughts and see what happens. At worst, you'll weaken a bond that wasn't authentic. At best, you'll find that you can disagree with someone and still be loved. This is the way to build genuine relationships instead of tentative, bartered alliances based on the currency of compliance.

These strategies won't eradicate your desire for approval or the anxiety you feel when disapproval comes your way. What they will do is give you practice accepting such desire and anxiety without relinquishing your integrity. Ironically, I've found that when I do this, I actually net more approval in the long run. I'm more fun to be around, and I do better work. I get happily lost in making my own kind of flawed and awkward music, music that always seems to sound sweetest in the moments I forget to care who's listening.

DECEMBER 2003

# How to Deal With Major Life Changes

......................................................

*What goes on in the cocoon of change isn't always pretty, but the results can be beautiful. Here are the four phases of human metamorphosis. Get ready to fly!*

......................................................

I used to think I knew how some caterpillars become butterflies. I assumed they weave cocoons, then sit inside growing six long legs, four wings, and so on. I figured if I were to cut open a cocoon, I'd find a butterfly-ish caterpillar, or a caterpillar-ish butterfly, depending on how far things had progressed. I was wrong. In fact, the first thing caterpillars do in their cocoons is shed their skin, leaving a soft, rubbery chrysalis. If you were to look inside the cocoon early on, you'd find nothing but a puddle of glop. But in that glop are certain cells, called imago cells, that contain the

DNA-coded instructions for turning bug soup into a delicate, winged creature—the angel of the dead caterpillar.

If you've ever been through a major life transition, this may sound familiar. Humans do it, too—not physically but psychologically. All of us will experience metamorphosis several times during our lives, exchanging one identity for another. You've probably already changed from baby to child to adolescent to adult—these are obvious, well-recognized stages in the life cycle. But even after you're all grown up, your identity isn't fixed. You may change marital status, become a parent, switch careers, get sick, win the lottery.

Any transition serious enough to alter your definition of self will require not just small adjustments in your way of living and thinking but a full-on metamorphosis. I don't know if this is emotionally stressful for caterpillars, but for humans it can be hell on wheels. The best way to minimize trauma is to understand the process.

## The Phases of Human Metamorphosis

Psychological metamorphosis has four phases. You'll go through these phases, more or less in order, after any major change catalyst (falling in love or breaking up, getting or losing a job, having children or emptying the nest, etc.). The strategies for dealing with change depend on the phase you're experiencing.

Phase One
# DISSOLVING

**HERE'S THE DEAL:** The first phase of change is the scariest, especially because we aren't taught to expect it. It's the time when we lose our identity and are left temporarily formless: person soup. Most people fight like crazy to keep their identities from dissolving. "This is just a blip," we tell ourselves when circumstances rock our world. "I'm the same person, and my life will go back to being the way it was."

Sometimes this is true. But in other cases, when real metamorphosis has begun, we run into a welter of "dissolving" experiences. We may feel that everything is falling apart, that we're losing everyone and everything. Dissolving feels like death, because it is—it's the demise of the person you've been.

**WHAT TO DO:** When we're dissolving we may get hysterical, fight our feelings, try to recapture our former lives, or jump immediately toward some new status quo ("rebound romance" is a classic example). All these measures actually slow down Phase One and make it more painful. The following strategies work better:

*In Phase 1, Live One Day (or 10 minutes) at a Time*
Instead of dwelling on hopes and fears about an unknowable future, focus your attention on whatever is happening right now.

## "Cocoon" by Caring For Yourself in Physical, Immediate Ways

Wrap yourself in a blanket, make yourself a cup of hot tea, attend an exercise class, whatever feels comforting.

## Talk to Others Who Have Gone Through a Metamorphosis

If you don't have a wise relative or friend, a therapist can be a source of reassurance.

## Let Yourself Grieve

Even if you are leaving an unpleasant situation (a bad marriage, a job you didn't like), you'll probably go through the normal human response to any loss: the emotional roller coaster called the grieving process. You'll cycle through denial, anger, sadness, and acceptance many times. Just experiencing these feelings will help them pass more quickly.

If you think this sounds frustratingly passive, you're right. Dissolving isn't something you do; it's something that happens to you. The closest you'll come to controlling it is relaxing and trusting the process.

Phase Two
# IMAGINING

**HERE'S THE DEAL:** For those of us who have just a few tiny control issues, Phase Two is as welcome as rain after drought. This is when the part of you that knows your destiny, the imago in your psyche, will begin giving you instructions about how to reorganize the remnants of your old identity into something altogether different.

The word imago is the root of the word image. You'll know you're beginning Phase Two when your mind's eye starts seeing images of the life you are about to create. These can't be forced—like dissolving, they happen to you—and they are never what you expected. You're becoming a new person, and you'll develop traits and interests your old self didn't have. You may feel compelled to change your hairstyle or wardrobe, or redecorate your living space. The old order simply seems wrong, and you'll begin reordering your outer situation to reflect your inner rebirth.

**WHAT TO DO:** Here are some ways you may want to respond when you begin spontaneously imagining the future:

## Cut Out Magazine Pictures You Find Appealing or Interesting
Glue them onto a piece of butcher paper. The resulting collage will be an illustration of the life you're trying to create.

*Let Yourself Daydream*

Your job is to try out imaginary scenarios until you have a clear picture of your goals and desires. You'll save a lot of time, effort, and grief by giving yourself time to do this in your head before you attempt it in the real world.

Phase Two is all about images: making them up, making them clear, and making them possible. Moving through this stage, you'll start to feel an impulse to go from dreaming (imagining possibilities) to scheming (planning to bring your vision to fruition). Write down both dreams and schemes, and then gather information about how you might create them.

## Phase Three
# RE-FORMING

**HERE'S THE DEAL:** As your dreams become schemes, you'll begin itching to make them come true. This signals Phase Three, the implementation stage of the change process. Phase Three is when you stop fantasizing about selling your art and start submitting work to galleries, or go beyond ogling a friend's brother to having her set you up on a date. You'll feel motivated to do real, physical things to build a new life. And then...(drum roll, please)...you'll fail. Repeatedly.

I've gone through Phase Three many times and watched hundreds of clients do the same. I've never seen a significant scheme succeed on the first try. Re-forming your life, like anything new, complex, and important, inevitably brings up problems you didn't expect. That's why, in contrast to the starry eyes that are so useful in Phase Two, Phase Three demands the ingenuity of Thomas Edison and the tenacity of a pit bull.

**WHAT TO DO:** *Expect things to go wrong.* Many of my clients have an early failure and consider this a sign that "it just wasn't meant to be." This is a useful philosophy if you want to spend your life as person soup. To become all that you can be, you must keep working toward your dreams even when your initial efforts are unsuccessful.

### Be Willing to Start Over

Every time your plans fail, you'll briefly return to Phase One, feeling lost and confused. This is an opportunity to release some of the illusions that created hitches in your plan.

### Revisit Phase 2

Adjusting your dreams and schemes to include the truths you've learned from your experimentation.

### Persist

Keep debugging and reimplementing your new-and-improved plans until they work. If you've followed all the steps above, they eventually will.

Phase Four
# FLYING

**HERE'S THE DEAL:** Phase Three is like crawling out of your cocoon and waiting for your crumpled, soggy wings to dry and expand. Phase Four is the payoff, the time when your new identity is fully formed and able to fly.

**WHAT TO DO:** The following strategies—which can help you optimize this delightful situation—are about fine-tuning, not drastic transformation

## Enjoy!
You've just negotiated a scary and dramatic transformation, and you deserve to savor your new identity. Spend time every day focusing on gratitude for your success.

## Make Small Improvements
Find little ways to make your new life a bit less stressful, a bit more pleasurable.

## Know That Another Change is Just Around the Bend
There's no way to predict how long you'll stay in Phase Four; maybe days, maybe decades. Don't attribute your happiness to your new identity; security lies in knowing how to deal with metamorphosis, whenever it occurs.

JANUARY 2004

# You Spot It, You've Got It

*"My friend is lazy, willful, and self-absorbed."*
*Wait—could that actually be me I'm talking about?*
*Here's what we can learn about ourselves from*
*the funny little phenomenon called projection.*

"There are two kinds of people I can't stand," says Michael Caine's character in the epically low comedy *Goldmember*, "those who are intolerant of other cultures, and the Dutch." I love this line, not because it slams the Dutch (for whom I feel great admiration) but because it slams hypocrisy—specifically, the baffling double standards of people who condemn in others the very offenses they themselves are committing. My fellow life coach Sharon Lamm calls this the "you spot it, you got it" syndrome. In other words, whatever we criticize most harshly in others may be a hallmark of our own psyche; what I hate most in you may actually be what I hate most in me.

This style of thinking is so illogical, you'd think it would be rare. Because of the peculiarities of human psychology, though, it's actually more the rule than the exception. Understanding the "you spot it, you got it" phenomenon requires some focused thinking, but the effort will bring more peace and sanity to your relationships and your inner life.

## When We Spot What We Got

Let's start by replicating a little thought experiment devised by psychologist Daniel Wegner: For the next 30 seconds, don't think about anything connected to the subject of white bears. Don't think about bears of any kind—or the Arctic, or snowy terrain, or white fur coats, etc. Ready? Go.

You probably just had more bear-related thoughts than you typically would in a month of Sundays. They're still coming, aren't they? You may distract yourself for an instant, but then another pops into your mind—see? There's one now!

This is a universal truth: We invariably experience more of any thought or feeling we try to avoid. Why? Because when our brains hear the instruction to shun a certain topic, they respond by seeking any thoughts related to that topic, in order to escape them. (After all, if you decided to throw away every blue thing in your closet, the first step would be to go looking for blue items, right?) Wegner calls this search the "ironic monitoring process," which has the perfect acronym: "imp." When we try to repress awareness of anything, we activate a mind imp that zeroes in on every memory, every sense impression, every experience related to the forbidden subject.

The "you spot it, you got it" phenomenon occurs when we do things that are in opposition to our own value systems. To feel good about acting in ways that are reprehensible to ourselves, we must repress our recognition that we're doing so. Our imps go into high gear; we become hyper alert to anything that reminds us of the behavior we're denying in ourselves, focusing with unusual intensity on the slightest hint of that behavior in others, or imagining it where it doesn't even exist.

This is why people can, without irony, say things like "So help me, Billy, if you keep hitting people, I will slap you into Thursday!" Or "I only lie to him because he's so dishonest." Condemning others for our worst traits turns us into ethical pretzels, hiding from us the very things we must change to earn genuine self-respect. Articulating such false logic is the key to resolving it—but this is always easier when we're talking about someone besides ourselves. So let's start there.

## Project And Reject: The Hypocrite's Two-Step

When we're the ones doing the spot-it-got-it tango, we don't see the paradox; we simply feel an unusually ferocious antipathy to someone else's actions. When someone else is perpetrating the very acts they claim to despise, we may feel confused, sensing that there's something crazy going on, unable to pinpoint exactly what. I have some recommendations.

### Be Suspicious. Be Very Suspicious

One of the friskiest babysitters I ever hired was a sweet little grandma I'll call Beulah. Despite her age, Beulah had endless energy; she could keep up with my three preschoolers far longer than I could. She was also touchingly concerned that my children not become "addicted" to anything: Sesame Street, ice cream, pop music. She volunteered to police my bathroom cupboards and remove any leftover medication the children might consume. Even so, she worried constantly that they would get drugs somewhere.

One day I came home from work to discover that Beulah had wallpapered half my daughter's bedroom with hideous paper she'd found at a discount store. She'd also single-handedly moved our piano to a new location, and (though I wouldn't discover this until weeks later) ordered four hundred dollars' worth of Girl Scout Cookies at my expense. As Beulah gave me a disjointed, rambling explanation at a rate of approximately 900 words per minute, I noted her many small scabs and that her pupils were dilated. I recalled an article that mentioned these were symptoms of crystal meth abuse. The light finally dawned: Beulah was a speed freak.

As I regretfully fired my babysitter, I realized that her obsessive talk about addiction had always been a "you spot it, you got it" behavior, and it should have been a signal to me that Beulah herself was a drug-stealing addict. Everyone makes comments about other people from time to time, but those who focus on one topic continually, irrationally, and inexplicably are often describing themselves. When someone seems unduly preoccupied with a certain flaw in others, it's time to do a once-over to see if it's taken root in Mr. or Ms. Obsessed.

## Sidestep Mind-Binds

If you want to experience insanity, observe a relationship with a hypocrite: the unfaithful lover who sees endless evidence of a partner's nonexistent infidelity; the rude, hurtful coworker who expects to be treated with kindness and respect; the political extremist who violently opposes violence. Opposite moral imperatives that come from the same person, called double binds, are so crazy-making that they were once thought to induce schizophrenia. If you try to have a close connection with someone who vehemently attacks flaws in others while demanding that you accept, overlook, or excuse those same flaws in him or her, you will feel a blend of anxiety, extreme bafflement, self-blame, anger, and hopelessness. When you see people abiding by a big fat double standard, step outside their duplicitous perspective by telling yourself that the craziness you feel is coming from the critic. Once you've had this perceptual breakthrough, you may be able to use it on the one person whose behavior you actually can change: yourself.

## See It And Free It

The impish nature of our psychology ensures that we all occasionally spot what we've got. However, we rarely see our own delusion; we just find ourselves ruminating on the vices of others. If Joe weren't so lazy, we think, he'd always bring me breakfast in bed. Or Chris is such a miser. Expected me to split the check for coffee—like I'm made of money! When these thoughts become especially dominant, there's a high probability we've got what we spot. But we can turn our own unconscious hypocrisy into a wonderful tool for personal growth. Here's how:

*Phase One: Write Your Rant*
To begin, list all the nasty, judgmental thoughts you're already thinking about Certain People. Who's offending you most right now? What do you hate most about them? What dreadful things have they done to you? What behavior should they change? Scribble down all your most controlling, accusatory, politically incorrect thoughts.

*Phase Two: Change Places*
Now go through your written rant and put yourself in the place of the person you're criticizing. Read through it again, and be honest—could it be that your enemy's shoe fits your own foot? If you wrote "Kristin always wants things her way," could "I always want things my way" be equally true? Could it be that this is the very reason Kristin's selfishness

bothers you so much? If you wrote "Joe has got to stop cling-ing and realize that our relationship is over," could it be that you are also hanging on to the relationship—say, by brood-ing all day about Joe's clinginess?

Sometimes you'll swear you don't see in yourself the loathsome qualities you notice in others. You spot it, but you ain't got it. Look again. See if you are implicitly condon-ing someone else's vileness by failing to oppose it—which puts your actions on the side of the trait you hate. You may be facilitating your boss's combativeness by bowing your head and taking it, rather than speaking up or walking out. Maybe you hate a friend's greediness, all the while "virtu-ously" allowing her to grab more than her share. Indirectly you are serving the habits you despise. Your rant rewrite may look like this example from one of my clients, Lenore:

### Phase One: The Rant
*"My kids take me for granted. They expect me to drop whatever I'm doing and focus on them, anytime. I'm sick of them taking me for granted."*

### Phase Two: The Rewrite
*"I take me for granted. I expect me to drop whatever I'm doing to focus on my kids, anytime. I'm sick of me taking me for granted."*

This exercise was a watershed for Lenore; once she realized that by devaluing herself she was teaching her children to devalue her, she could begin getting respect from them by respecting herself.

We can often learn such priceless lessons by remembering the "you spot it, you got it" dynamic. Recognizing this impish quirk of human thinking helps us peacefully detach from crazy-makers who might otherwise drive us nuts, and jolts us free from the places we get most stuck. We automatically become freer, less caught in illusion, less obsessed with other people's flaws. That's good, because there's nothing worse than people who are always talking about what they hate in other people. Boy, do I hate them.

JULY 2004

# How to Think Your Way Free

................................................................

*Wait—you can transform your life by altering your thoughts? Believe it. Here is the mood-altering, immunity-bolstering, luck-making impact of changing your mind.*

................................................................

O kay, this time you're serious. You're going on a regimen that will really improve your health—not like that crash diet: You'll snarf down antioxidants; exercise moderately but consistently; balance fats, proteins, and carbs; and pay attention to the way you explain whatever happens to you.

Wait a minute. The way you explain what happens? What does that have to do with physical health? According to findings from the burgeoning field of behavioral medicine, a lot. How we think can affect physical processes as surely as diet and exercise do. For example, putting a positive spin on events in our past is associated with an enormous array of health benefits, from improved immune function to reduced stress to quicker healing, with all their emotional and physical advantages. To some degree, we may be able to literally explain away many devastating physical problems. If you want to have a healthier body, I suggest changing your mind first.

## So What's Your Story?

Caroline, one of my brightest, prettiest, best-educated clients, was a wreck. Her pet cockatiel, Bonkers, had flown away.

The way she told the story of her bird's disappearance—what researchers have called "explanatory style"—was making her situation much worse. Her explanation of Bonkers' great escape showed the three key markers of pessimism: She described the problem as being personal ("I made it happen; these things always happen to me"), permanent ("Things will never get better"), and pervasive ("My whole life is rotten; I'm such a loser").

On the other hand, I'd noticed that whenever something good happened, she explained it as a fluke. " This cute guy from work asked me out," she said one day. Caroline explained the man's interest in her as his own "insanity" (not personal) and assumed it wouldn't last (not permanent). She stressed that other people's interest never lasted, even though I knew she had been the one to end most romantic relationships (not pervasive).

Bear in mind that Caroline didn't think like this only when she talked to me. Day in, day out, her mind serialized every piece of bad luck into another episode in a continuing Saga of Doom and deflected every happy event into the Meaningless Trivia scrap pile. Her style was crushing her mood—and was probably damaging her body as well.

## Why See the Glass Half Empty?

Despite its attendant miseries, there seems to be a useful place for a pessimistic explanatory style. Some people appear to downplay positive aspects of their situations to limit their expectations and help them feel less pressured. They're less likely to feel let down if things go wrong.

Researchers Julie Norem and Nancy Cantor call this defensive pessimism. My friend Julia calls it inoculating yourself against disappointment. In the seven years I've known her, Julia has changed her explanatory style deliberately, gradually, and successfully. Giving up defensive pessimism may invite disappointment in certain situations, but overall, Julia's quality of life and her physical health are benefiting as she turns herself into a thoroughgoing optimist.

This doesn't happen overnight. If you're a habitual pessimist, you know there's nothing worse than those bouncy optimists.

Habitual thought patterns are like ruts in a dirt road. The mind slips into them over and over, and at first, steering down another route is extremely difficult. Stopping habitual thoughts as they flash along these pathways, turning one's mental energy to a new way of thinking, requires an effort that is not merely impressive but heroic.

## How to Change Your Mind

I've said it before, and I'll say it again: The way to start changing your mind is not to force it or command it but to watch it. Jeffrey Schwartz, MD, who studies obsessive-compulsive disorders, teaches his patients "mindful awareness," a form of meditation that can free them from intrusive thoughts— a technique that has also been shown to help other patients stop a blue mood from becoming full-blown depression. The idea is to identify a destructive thought pattern, then simply label it and watch it and let it pass by whenever it appears in your mind.

When Caroline did this, her mood changed immediately. Instead of drowning in thoughts like "Bonkers never loved me!" she learned to say, "Oh look, there's a pessimistic explanation." This gave her enough space, enough mental distance, to at least consider a more optimistic story.

If you want to change your explanatory style, start by evaluating where you fall on the spectrum from pessimism to optimism. Researchers do this by analyzing the way people use the "three Ps" (personal, permanent, and pervasive elements) in their descriptions of past events. (You can use this quiz, www.oprah.com/spirit/Whats-Your-Explanatory-Style-A-Quiz.) Unless your score shows you to be wildly optimistic, consider nudging yourself further toward the bright side.

Testing your explanatory style is the beginning of mindfulness (page 67), of watching the way your brain tells stories. Initially, you may simply notice that a thought seems negative; as you pay more attention, you will begin to see how you use the three Ps.

Once you've become aware of your explanatory style and its elements, make a concerted effort to describe positive events as personal, permanent, and pervasive. Tell the story of a bad event without personalizing it or thinking that it will have a broad, lasting impact on your life.

## Staying the Course

The great thing about developing an optimistic explanatory style is that it's self-reinforcing. It increases your hope and expectation that your whole health-and-fitness regimen, mental and physical, will be worth the effort. This frame of mind will help keep you not only happy but healthy; studies have linked it to improved immune function, better lung function, quicker recovery from heart surgery, and a lower risk of heart disease. I've also noticed that it correlates with my clients' ability to achieve all their goals. Changing your thought diet—your way of thinking—may be the best thing you can do to stay on your food diet.

I suspect this is why Caroline, like many of my clients who successfully change their explanatory patterns, has experienced an unexpected side effect: She's in the best shape of her life. She's managed to drop a pattern of emotional eating, stay on an effective workout schedule, and lose five pounds. Even more dramatic are the changes in her posture and facial expression, which have gone from cringing and miserable to alert and interested, making her much more attractive and approachable. Not only does her mood improve every time she observes and alters a negative explanation rather than getting mired in it, but her body appears to love the change.

And I suggest that Caroline can expect this trend to continue. Is this an optimistic explanation? You bet. I'm sticking to my diet.

AUGUST 2004

## *Mindfulness with Martha Beck*

*A few minutes of alone time can save your sanity. I can't live without this simple meditation practice called "Mindfulness." Use it when your attention is scattered. It will bring you back to a calm state and allow your brain to function normally.*

**STEP 1:** Start by sitting in a way that doesn't block anything: sit with your legs uncrossed and with your hands resting on your legs.

**STEP 2:** Become aware of the feeling in your toes. Wiggle them and feel the texture of your socks.

**STEP 3:** Now move that feeling up to your legs and calves.

**STEP 4:** Close your eyes and breathe in. Visualize air going into your body and traveling down into your legs and feet. This air is going to clean away all of the tension.

**STEP 5:** As you breathe out, visualize all of your tension as a dark cloud that that you just blow out into the air.

# You Have The Right To Remain Silent

........................................................................................

*Your cell phone is ringing. Your inbox is overflowing. Your friend wants to discuss her son's glue-sniffing habit. Here's some news for you—you don't have to be there for all people all the time. Just follow these escape routes.*

........................................................................................

y thesis: The great English writer E.M. Forster may have valued connection above all else, but for us 21st-century folks—with our jam-packed Rolodexes, e-mail from intimates and strangers, phone messages left by friends, colleagues, passing acquaintances, and the occasional deranged stalker—disconnection is as necessary as connection for creating a healthy, happy life. When we force ourselves to connect against our heart's desires, we create false, resentful relationships; when we disconnect from the people who deplete us, we set them free to find their tribes while we find ours. I planned to illustrate these thoughts with snippets of Greek philosophy, and perhaps even the poetry of Robert Frost.

But it has just occurred to me that this refined approach is not how I actually disconnect—and I need to disconnect a lot. Overconnection is my major occupational hazard. My job is all about soulfully linking with others, and this is truly as much fun as I've ever had with my clothes on, but after doing this with many people for many hours, I often feel as if I've watched ten great movies back-to-back: dazed, frazzled, longing for silent solitude. I'm not up to gracious separation; I need quick-and-dirty ways to save my sanity, right now.

So I've listed some of my favorite disconnection strategies below, in the hope that you might find them useful. Please remember that this advice is not for the E.M. Forsters of the world but for those of us who are already connected up the wazoo.

*I. **HIDE.*** I'm sitting in my room at a beautiful wilderness retreat where intelligent, sensitive, wonderful people come to renew their spirits. I've been running a workshop meant to stir the deepest reaches of the participants' fears and dreams. I've also been living on tap water and protein bars because the thought of going to the dining hall, where I would end up connecting for another hour with those intelligent, sensitive, wonderful people, makes me want to shoot myself.

I packed for this trip with disconnection aforethought, tossing in 20 protein bars with the express intention of hiding out. Blame my high school English teacher—I'll call her Mrs. Jensen—who married at 17, bore her first child at 19, and was a farmwife and mother of four by age 22. When she felt overwhelmed, she'd retreat into a field of tall corn near her house and hide there, listening to her children search for her, until she heard a cry of genuine pain or felt ready to reconnect, whichever came first.

"Martha," Mrs. Jensen told me, "every woman needs a cornfield. No matter what's happening in your life, find yourself a cornfield and hide there whenever you need to."

All these years later, this advice still gives me permission to sit here by myself contemplating whether I should eat the nondairy creamer from my in-room coffee setup, just for variety. I've used hundreds of other "cornfields" over the years: cars, forests, hotels, bathrooms. I've been known to hide for days, but even a few minutes can calm my strung-out nerves—or yours. If you don't already have a cornfield, find one now.

**2. GO PRIMITIVE.** We all know that technological advances have made connection easier than ever before. They've also led some people to think that breaking away is a violation of the social order. Friends call to chastise each other (well, anyway, my friends call to chastise me) for being slow to return text messages or e-mail, as though the ability to communicate in half a dozen newfangled ways makes constant attention to every one of them morally imperative.

At such times, I become downright Amish, religiously committed to avoiding all modern communication technology. I unplug phones, computers, intercoms, and fax machines, risking opprobrium because I know that if I don't lose touch with some of the people who are trying to reach me, I'll lose touch with myself. The overconnected me is a cranky, tired fussbudget. Silence is golden if it keeps me from broadcasting that fretful self into my network of treasured relationships.

**3. PLAY FAVORITES.** Your ability to connect is a resource much more precious than money, so manage it well. Make a list of everyone to whom you feel bonded, then consider what kind of return you're getting on your investment. Which relationships make you feel robbed or depleted? Which ones enrich you? Notice that there are many ways for "connection investments" to pay off. One person may be good at helping you solve relationship problems, while another can fix your home computer and another makes you laugh. A baby's trust may be the only return you get on a massive investment of time and energy, but it can feel like winning the lottery.

It may sound cold-blooded to say you must divest yourself of the relationships that give you consistent losses, but unless you do this, you'll soon run out of capital, and you'll have no connection energy left to invest in anybody. So please, decide now to deliberately limit the time and attention you spend on "low yield" relationships. Above all...

**4. GET RID OF SQUID.** Squid is my word for people who seem to be missing their backbones but possess myriad sucking tentacles of emotional need. Like many invertebrates, squid appear limp and squishy—but once they get a grip on you, they're incredibly powerful. Masters at catalyzing guilt and obligation, they operate by squeezing pity from everyone they meet. They can make you feel entwined to the point of rage, desperate to escape their clutches, unable to see a means to extricate yourself.

Getting a squid out of your life is never pretty. (Excuses don't work—tell a squid you're on your way to a colonoscopy, and they'll come along to sit beside you, complaining, while your doctor performs the procedure.) Since you can't make a graceful exit, don't try. Scrape off squid any way you can. Tell them straightforwardly that you want them, yes them, to leave now, yes, now. This will be unpleasant. There will be lasting hurt feelings. Don't worry. Squid love hurt feelings. They hoard them, trading them in for pity points when they find another victim—er, friend. Let them go, their coffers bulging.

**5. BE INSENSITIVE.** A friend I'll call Zoe once went to a world-famous psychologist to discuss her recurring nightmares.

After months of waiting for an appointment, she finally met the therapist, who asked why she had come.

"I'm having terrible dreams," Zoe explained.

"Yeah?" grunted the famous psychologist. "So what?"

Zoe blinked, then stammered, "Well, they keep me awake."

"Uh-huh. So?"

"Well...," stammered Zoe, "I guess I never thought of it that way." And her nightmares went away, never to return. Once she stopped treating bad dreams like the end of the world, her mind had no reason to replay them.

I'm not suggesting that you say "So what?" every time someone turns to you for help, but I like to think that therapist was famous for a reason. I suspect he could feel the difference between something that required deep discussion and something that didn't. He was willing to be insensitive, alerting Zoe to her own hypersensitivity.

This is a very compassionate way to use your own psychological instincts. Instead of connecting with every person's problems, let yourself feel whether someone really needs your attention, or whether the best gift you can give might be a little abruptness.

**6. REHEARSE ESCAPE LINES.** When I'm overextended, I paradoxically become worse at setting boundaries. I end up resorting to rehearsed exit lines. "Oh, there's my doorbell!" I might say to end a client call that's run 20 minutes over (this is technically true: My doorbell is, in fact, there). When someone collars me in an airport, eager to share personal problems and ask for solutions, I may point behind them and say, "Oh, my gosh! Is that Dr. Phil?" Then, when their head snaps around, owl-like, I sprint for the nearest restroom.

I'm sure you can come up with better getaway lines than these, but do take the time to rehearse several reliable alternatives. Because when you're exhausted, a practiced excuse can keep you from wading deeper into relationships you don't need and can't handle.

**7. BE SHALLOW.** Even staying in touch with a reasonably small number of high-quality people can be overwhelming if you tend toward emotional intensity. In such cases, shallowness can be a delightful alternative. So instead of discussing Schopenhauer with your beloved in meaningful, calligraphed epistles, e-mail a stupid joke. Gather your friends to watch TV shows in which strangers paint one another's rooms the color of phlegm and then feign mutual delight. Once you know you can swim in the deep end of human connection, it's fun to splash around in the shallows.

I hope you find these disconnection strategies as useful as I do. By striking a balance between the imperative to "only connect" and the need for individuation, you really will relax your psyche and your relationships, making your life as a whole more joyful, more loving. Maybe someday we'll meet to compare notes, to share disconnection experiences as well as time, space, and perhaps a protein bar. But right now, I'm sure you'll understand when I say that I'd like to eat this one all by myself.

DECEMBER 2004

# I Love You Just the Way You Were

*You've lost weight. Or you're marrying the man of your dreams. Or you're studying Chinese and planning a trip to Beijing. Why is everybody in your life acting so weird? Here are some tips on how to deal with the people who just can't let go of the old you.*

I magine this: You're putting together a nifty jigsaw puzzle—say, your favorite Elvis montage painting on black velvet—when one of the pieces suddenly morphs into an entirely different shape. Aside from the unnerving quantum-mechanical implications of this event, you've got a problem—the surrounding pieces no longer fit. You could try to alter those pieces (a troubling prospect, since it will require distorting all the ones around them) or give up on the puzzle entirely—unless, of course, you could get the little sucker to resume its former shape and size.

This sort of situation arises in every human life. We live in social systems—families and neighborhoods, offices and nations—that call for continuous, complex interconnection. Any person who undergoes a dramatic shift creates a ripple effect, requiring change from others around her. The fact that you're reading this suggests that you're inclined toward personal growth. I'm guessing you've been this way for years, whether it's a trait you celebrate every day or a dirty secret you ruminate over while churning butter with your Amish kinfolk. The problem, as you may have noticed, is that not everyone you know, love, or work with is overjoyed to tread the path of change along with you.

Because we are a species that fears the unknown, most people reject the continuous transformation that is human reality and try to lock others into predictable behavior. "Promise me that you'll never change," lovers whisper to one another, though only a model from Madame Tussauds Wax Museum could keep such an enormous promise. In short, anyone who thinks new thoughts or does new deeds is likely to garner disapproval and criticism from someone.

## How to Handle a Change-Back Attack

Women who are undergoing changes are likely to experience "change back" messages from their nearest and dearest. The messages come in many forms: sabotage, cold silence, shouted insults, refusal to cooperate. But all convey just one idea: "I don't like what you've done. Go back to being the way you were." This might seem baffling in the face of positive achievements like losing weight, falling in love, or learning new ideas.

But change-back attackers aren't really thinking about the person they're pressuring. They're fighting for their lives—or at least life as they know it. These people are motivated not only by their own fear of change but by the pressure of other "puzzle pieces" that surround them. The force of a change-back attack has the weight of all those relationships. Resist successfully, and you may end up affecting people you'll never meet.

First, a basic attitude adjustment: Most people who are on the receiving end of change-back messages go into fits of guilt or defensiveness, then revert to familiar behaviors. This, of course, is exactly what the disgruntled party wants. Part of every personal evolution strategy should be a determination to greet these messages with pride and joy, as a sure sign you're making progress. Call a friend, a therapist, a fellow self-improvement devotee, and report the good news: "Guess what? I just got six blowbacks in one conversation! I must really be making progress!" Once you've made this attitudinal shift, you're ready for a systematic defense.

## Begin Your Systematic Defense

*Step 1: Pay respectful attention.*
When someone launches a change-back attack against you, refrain from resisting or submitting; just pay attention. Remember that whether you realize it or not, your actions may be forcing this friend to either make personal alterations or give up on "fitting" with you. Noticing their fear may calm you, and this may go a long way toward calming them.

If someone comes at you with a direct, obstreperous argument, try these unexpected, attentive responses: "Tell me." "I'm listening." "I hear you." "Say a little bit more on that." Attentiveness is a mobile, fluid stance that allows you to observe and respond without sustaining much damage. As Mark Twain said about doing right, it will gratify some people and astonish the rest.

*Step 2: Take time to find your truth.*
So you've paid attention. You know that the bag of bacon cheeseburgers on the table is just evidence that your loving husband is afraid he'll lose you. You've listened calmly as your angry teenager or judgmental parent lambasted you for your new achievements. Find a private moment for yourself. Now breathe and relax. Recall the chain of events that motivated your metamorphosis in the first place: the fat, the loneliness, the illumination. Honestly consider the feedback

you've just received. Maybe it feels absolutely right; if so, reverse course. Maybe it's partly right. Fine, alter your direction. Or maybe the complaint is just plain wrong. In that case, you must keep going, trusting that the best gift you can offer others is the resolute embrace of your own truth.

## Step 3: State your position for the record.

If your change-back attacker is sober and in a reasonably receptive frame of mind, you may want to respond to her argument. Even when you're dealing with a nasty, non-communicative person, stating your position may be a powerful step in your own development. It may not make the slightest impression on your unrelenting foes, but hearing the truth spoken in your own voice can clear your head and buoy your heart, at which point you'll have won the battle.

## Vanquish Your Change-Back Attackers

## Step 4: Unconditional Love

There's a secret weapon in the change wars, one that can fill the gaps and soften the edges of our constantly morphing identities—and I don't mean leaving your whole social system or forcing others to conform to you at every moment in time. The answer is unconditional love, and I encourage you to use it with ruthless abandon.

You'll know you've vanquished your change-back attackers when you can love them completely without agreeing with them at all. You can't force this feeling—it will happen naturally when you're ready—but when it strikes, express it, without acquiescing to others' verbal jabs. Doing this cheerfully and unabashedly will confound your average saboteurs by giving them nothing to oppose.

At best, this approach will cause your adversaries to stop, ponder, and perhaps feel less scared of making their own improvements. At worst, it will render you flexible, able to fit in with many people and social systems without getting stuck in any one position. The more you claim your own destiny, the easier it will be to love unconditionally. The more you love, the more comfortably you'll fit in with all sorts of people. Ultimately, situations that once brought on horrendous change-back attacks, that once appeared to you as utterly unworkable puzzles, may end up barely fazing you at all.

MAY 2005

# Four Steps to Find Your Life's Path

### Step One
### GET STILL

*Why Become Still?*

Inner stillness is the key factor for "hearing" our best lives calling to us. Of course, if we can't get still, our lives still communicate with us, but they often have to shout with such deafening voices that we can't ignore them. Our true selves are always whispering instructions about what we should do next, whether that's changing the world or just changing our attitudes. If we're still enough to hear our own inner voices at this subtle, almost silent level, we tend to choose the course through life that feels most blessed and least traumatic.

## Obstacles to Getting Still

If you've recently suffered pain, loss, or great confusion, becoming still may feel threatening. Many of us sustain a high level of mental "noise" so that we won't fully experience the difficult emotions of fear, anger, or sadness. Getting still requires being willing to experience these feelings without doing anything in the short run. You don't have to do anything in the stillness except fully acknowledge what you are feeling, without judgment. You'll find that if you can sit still with strong emotion for just a few minutes, even the worst emotional pain rises, crests, breaks, and recedes like a wave on the surf. Staying mentally and physically still as we watch this process gives us the experience and courage to face whatever our lives may bring. Here's how to get still, if you're unfamiliar with the process.

## How to Get Still

Fortunately, stillness is not a feat of mental discipline available only to meditation masters. It begins with concrete, physical behavior. The first is simply to sit or lie down without moving; the second is to breathe. This is so simple (though not always easy) that it's hard to believe how central it is to inner peace and the ability to navigate safely through life. Neuroscientists now know that breathing patterns change our brain states, allowing us to create—simply by inhaling and exhaling—the calm and peace necessary to survive difficult circumstances.

Try this now: Sit with your spine as straight as possible. Imagine that you're suspended from a string attached to the crown of your head; then picture that string dropping down through your spinal column as a thin, bright beam of light. Keep your back and neck aligned so the light finds its way through the core of your spinal column.

Next, breathe in so deeply that your entire torso expands outward. Fill your lungs, but also drop your diaphragm so that your belly expands (you can suck in your gut again as soon as the exercise is over). Completely empty your body of air when you exhale, then watch your body spontaneously decide when and how fast to inhale again. Continue to watch this process until you realize that you are not so much breathing as "being breathed." Your body knows its right pattern of oxygenation—you don't have to figure it out or do anything to make it happen.

Watch your body breathe seven or eight times, allowing yourself to observe any emotion or thought that comes to mind, without trying to stop it. You'll soon see that the mind thinks the way the lungs breathe—on its own. As you notice this, you will have achieved a measure of distance from both body and mind. You will be in the still place at the center of consciousness from which your true self is always whispering to you.

## Step Two
# KNOW THE TRUTH

*What Does "Know the Truth" Mean?*

This step doesn't require that you achieve some philosophical epiphany about All Truth Everywhere. It simply means that you must be able to consciously acknowledge what is happening to you, and what is happening within you—your life circumstances and the thoughts and feelings you have that relate to those life circumstances.

There are many aspects of the truth we hide from ourselves, because they would make us uncomfortable or necessitate change. Hidden truth actually cements negative situations in place. At the moment we finally own our truth, almost miraculously, positive change begins. The truth really does set us free. That's why an alcoholic begins recovery the moment he or she says, "I'm an alcoholic." It's also why your life can only begin to work well if you acknowledge that some of your efforts are failing, or that you simply don't feel good about them.

*Obstacles to Knowing the Truth*

It's peculiar that we can hide from truths we already know, yet we do it every day. You may tell others you feel "fine" (in fact, you may think it's true), when you're actually tired, sad, or angry. You may pretend to be comfortable in an uncomfortable situation in order to make social interactions run more smoothly. Or you may "go blind" to someone's immoral or cruel behavior because you desperately want to believe that person is wholly good. Most of all, you may hide from the truth because once it's out in the open, it will cause your life to change. That's always scary—but spoken truths always cause change that is positive in the long run, even if it's frightening at first. Opening up about your anger toward someone who abused you, about your fear of aging, about the fact that your child is an addict, etc., etc., is the only way to conquer fear and begin healing everything that may be wounded in your life.

### How to Know the Truth

Once you've reached a place of inner stillness, get a pencil and paper and finish these statements:

*1. What I really don't want to know is that...*

*2. I'm avoiding looking at the fact that...*

*3. The absolute bottom-line truth about my life is...*

*4. The thing I'm avoiding thinking about is...*

If you have no unexamined thoughts, this won't be difficult; you may find only that your sweater is too scratchy or that your father's jokes are boring. But if you've suffered any of the slings and arrows of outrageous fortune, you may find anger, fear, or grief rising into consciousness as you dig up the raw truth. Don't be afraid of the feelings or thoughts that emerge—remain in stillness and they will soon lessen. Remember, you don't have to DO anything right now, you just have to see the truth of your life with an unsparingly honest eye.

Step Three
### FEEL YOUR SOUL'S DESIRES

*Why Is Knowing the Soul's Desires So Important?*
Many people go through life unwittingly expecting other people to figure out what makes them happy, and then give it to them. Anyone who's raised a baby knows that this is actually how we must care for our infants, and in some cases, the infant mentality never leaves. The problem is that others aren't mind readers, and even if they were, they could never fulfill your desires until you become fully aware of them. Again, many of us aren't aware of exactly what we want—we feel a vague sense of lack or jealousy about others' good fortune, or a kind of inner void that aches to be filled.

All of these symptoms are indicators that it's time to clarify and specify our soul's desires. My belief is that we already know these desires, and that recognizing them requires only one thing: We must stop listening so obsessively to our minds.

## Obstacles to Knowing the Soul's Desires

The biggest obstacle to a recognition of our soul's desires is the mind. Our minds are conditioned to think in narrow little patterns, usually established by our families and our culture. The soul tells us what we want and need, while the mind tells us what we *think* we want and need.

The soul knows, "I want freedom from worry," and the mind thinks, "I want to win the lottery." The soul knows, "I want to feel connected with all things," and the mind translates that to, "I need the perfect romantic soul mate to make me feel connected." The soul is always right. The mind is usually wrong. In stillness and truth, we can tell which is which. The truth of the soul resonates with a deep sense of passion and conviction. The mind's desires feel frantic, clinging, and grasping. Any hint of these desperate emotions is evidence that you're stuck on your mind's desires. Breathe deeply, let them go, and dig deeper to find your soul's desires. Here's one useful method:

## How to Know Your Soul's Desires

Get another piece of paper and write at the top, "Things I want." Then, list as many things as you can think of—a new car, a better job, thinner thighs, whatever. When you've listed everything you can think of, turn to a new page.

At the top of this page, write, "Things I yearn for." Then, start listing. You'll find yourself coming up with things that didn't appear on your first list, which was made mostly by your mind. We want cars—we yearn for freedom and mobility. We want hot sex—we yearn for intimacy. We want to be beautiful—we yearn for total self-acceptance. As you list the things your soul yearns for, let go of the need to figure out how they might be fulfilled. Your methods will probably not work—cars, sex, and beauty don't automatically lead to freedom, intimacy, and self-acceptance. Allow yourself to be okay with not knowing, for the present moment, how the universe intends to fulfill your soul's desires. The more you let go of the process, the sooner it will happen. *And it will happen.*

Step Four
## TRUST YOUR LIFE
## TO UNFOLD PERFECTLY

### Why Trust Is Crucial

The way to let go of your soul's desires, to achieve nonattachment, is not to go into "martyr mode" and expect a life of blunted appetites or unmet needs. Letting go is the natural result of trust—trust that the Force, or God, or whatever you want to call it, fulfills its own nature by answering your soul's requests, once you have articulated them. To sit patiently with a yearning that has not yet been fulfilled, and to trust that that fulfillment will come, is quite possibly one of the most powerful "magic skills" that human beings are capable of. It has been noted by almost every ancient wisdom tradition. If you can master it, you'll see your soul's desires being filled in ways that are often amazing, and sometimes flat-out miraculous.

## Obstacles to Trust

One morning during the Miraval Spa contest-winners' retreat, I knew all the women had received certificates telling them to come get a free outfit from New Balance. When I asked them how they liked their new outfits, I discovered that every woman in the room had thrown away the gift voucher, because they assumed they would be charged for the clothes.

This became a touchstone experience for me, one I've thought about a thousand times since. Here the universe, in the form of a generous company, was trying to give these women a beautiful, free gift, and they were turning away from it without even knowing it was being offered because of their assumption that it would cost too much. If they had trusted their own eyes, they would have seen that the outfit was a gift. Instead, they trusted their pain, their disappointment, their hard-knock lessons that life is difficult and nothing's free. We all have many such experiences. We take away assumptions that all of life is painful, and that we can expect the same bad treatment from the world we may have experienced in limited situations during our childhoods or difficult adult years.

## How to Trust

The inability to open up to hope is what blocks trust, and

blocked trust is the reason for blighted dreams. Begin to hope again, then trust that your soul's desires are meant to be fulfilled.

You can start this with something small as an experiment. Choose a soul's desire that seems modest, like the desire to smell flowers or hear music. Make sure you identify something that's really coming from your core, but make it something fairly modest. Then, deliberately choose to trust that your wish will be fulfilled. Feel so sure of it that you don't even need the outcome, because you feel as if you already have it. Then watch and see. Be open to all ways in which your answer may come. Your trust will be rewarded.

I'm confident saying this because I've worked with thousands of clients over the years, and I've seen how trust works. It may mean an unexpected visit from a loved one, a chance to relax and have a quiet cup of tea, an opportunity to start your own business, the gradual unfolding of a childhood ambition.

A final exercise: Right now, make a list of every desire of your soul that has been fulfilled in the past. Then, taking each fulfilled wish one by one, recall the coincidences, strokes of "luck," generosity from other people or inspired ideas that helped you fulfill that desire. You'll find that your life has already been a linked chain of miraculous delights. The Miraval winners received another link in the chain, but they have many, many more to come. And so do you.

# How to Be
# Wildly Successful

*If at first you don't succeed . . . ask yourself, Am I an otter? A squirrel? A mouse? The answer could spell the difference between things going swimmingly and squeaking to a halt. Find your own winning style.*

I t was a problem I'd never anticipated: My brainy daughter was having trouble in school. Katie began teaching herself to read at 15 months and tested at a "post–high school" level in almost every subject by fourth grade. Yet her middle-school grades were dropping like a lead balloon, and her morale along with them. I cared more about the morale than the grades. I knew Katie was quickly losing something educational psychologists call her sense of self-efficacy—her belief that she could succeed at specific tasks and life in general. People who lack this trait tend to stop trying because they expect to fail. Then, of course, they do fail, feel even worse, shut down even more, and carry on to catastrophe.

I couldn't understand what put Katie on this slippery slope. True, some people seem genetically inclined to believe in themselves—or not—but experience powerfully influences our sense of self-efficacy. I knew Katie had been confident as a preschooler, but her current trouble at school was destroying her optimism. I tried to help in every way I could. I created homework-checking systems, communicated with teachers like bosom buddies, doled out penalties and rewards. Mostly, though, I just kept cheering Katie on. I was sure that if she would stop hesitating, believe in herself, and just throw herself into the task at hand, she'd get past the problem.

Boy, was I ever wrong.

It took years of confidence-battering struggle—for both Katie and me—before I finally got the information I needed. It came from a no-nonsense bundle of kindly energy named Kathy Kolbe, a specialist on the instinctive patterns that shape human action. Kathy's father pioneered many standardized intelligence tests, but Kathy was born with severe dyslexia, which meant that this obviously bright little girl didn't learn in a typical way. She grew up determined to understand and defend the different ways in which people go about solving problems.

The day Katie and I met her, Kathy was wearing a T-shirt that said "do nothing when nothing works," a motto that typifies her approach. On her desk were the results from the tests (the Kolbe A and Y Indexes) that my daughter and I had just taken to evaluate our personal "conative styles," or typical action patterns.

"Well," said Kathy, glancing at a bar graph, "I see you both listen better when you're drawing."

Katie and I stared at each other, astonished. Bull's-eye.

"And you've both had a zillion teachers tell you to stop drawing. They said you could do only one thing at a time, but that's not true for you two, is it? You have a hard time focusing if there's nothing to occupy your eyes and hands."

Unexpectedly, I found myself tearing up with gratitude. I'd never realized how frustrated I'd been by the very situation Kathy was describing. Katie sat up a little straighter in her chair.

"But," Kathy went on, "Martha, you go about problem-solving in a different way from Katie. There are four basic action modes, and you're what I call a Quick Start. When you want to learn, you just jump in and start messing around."

Another bull's-eye. I cannot count the times I've been defeated, humiliated, or physically injured immediately after saying the words, "Hey, how hard can it be?" But that never seems to stop me from saying them again.

"Now," Kathy went on, "Katie's not a Quick Start. She's a Fact Finder. Before she starts a task, she needs to know all about it. She needs to go through the instructions and analyze them for flaws, then get more information to fill in the gaps."

To my amazement, my daughter nodded vigorously. I've never understood why some people hesitate before diving into unfamiliar tasks or activities. I couldn't imagine wanting more instructions about anything.

"There are two other typical patterns," Kathy explained. "The people I call Implementors—like Thomas Edison, for example—need physical objects to work with. They figure out things by building models or doing concrete tasks. Then there are the Follow Thrus. They set up orderly systems, like the Dewey decimal system or a school curriculum.

"And that, Katie," she said, "is why you're having trouble. The school system was created mainly by people who are natural Follow Thrus. It works best for students with the same profile. Your teachers want you to fit into the system, but you have a hard time seeing how it works. If you question the instructions—which you absolutely need to do—they think you're being sassy."

Katie nodded so hard I feared for her cervical vertebrae. I was stunned. I'd spent years trying to understand my daughter, and a veritable stranger had just nailed the problem in ways I'd never even conceptualized. Katie wanted more instructions? You could have knocked me down with a feather.

## Basic Instinct

I've told this story in detail because since meeting Kathy, studying her work, and seeing how dramatically it affects people and their productivity, I've become convinced that many of us feel like failures because we don't recognize (let alone accept) that our instinctive methods of acting are as varied as our eye color. Our modus operandi shapes the way we do everything: make breakfast, drive, learn math. Not recognizing natural differences in our conative styles— assuming instead that we're idiots because we do things unconventionally—can destroy that precious sense of self-efficacy.

Imagine a race between four animals: an otter, a mole, a squirrel, and a mouse. They're headed for a goal several feet away. Which animal will win? Well, it depends. If the goal is underground, my money's on the mole. If it's in a tree? Hello, Mr. Squirrel. Underwater, it's the otter. And if the goal is hidden in tall grass, the mouse will walk away with it. Now, all these animals can swim, dig, climb, and find things in the grass. It's just that each of them does one of these things better than the others. Putting all four animals in a swimming race, say, would lead to the conclusion that one was better than the others, when the truth is simply that their innate skills are different.

If we're in an environment (such as school, a job, or a family tradition) that asks us to act against our natural style, we feel uncomfortable at best, tormented at worst. Even if we manage to conform, we don't get a high sense of self-efficacy because although we've managed the efficacy part of the equation, we've lost the self. When we fail, we feel like losers; when we succeed, we feel like impostors.

Thanks to Kathy's work (and centuries of psychological work on conation), I've stopped asking others to match my instinctive style. I no longer expect squirrels to swim and otters to climb trees. As a result, I'm better able to support myself, my children, and everyone else I know. Here's a quick primer on how you can do the same:

## Accept that you have an inborn, instinctive style of action

Just learning that there are four distinct patterns of action was a huge aha for me. When Katie and I accepted that we simply had different ways of doing things, our relationship and her confidence began to improve immediately. To identify your own action-mode profile, you can take a formal online test (the Kolbe Index at kolbe.com; there is a charge), or just observe your own approach to getting something done. To give you an example, people with different profiles might respond to a challenge—let's say, learning to crochet—in the following ways:

> *Quick Start: If you're a Quick Start who wants to crochet, you'll probably buy some yarn and a hook, get*

a few tips from an experienced crochetmeister, and jump right into trial and error.

**Fact Finder:** *You'll spend hours reading, watching, asking questions, and learning about crocheting before actually beginning to use the tools.*

**Implementor:** *You pay less attention to words than to concrete objects, so you might draw a pattern of a crochet stitch or even create a large model using thick rope, before you go near a needle.*

**Follow Thru:** *You'll likely schedule a lesson with a crochet teacher or buy a book that proceeds through a yarn curriculum, learning new stitches in order of difficulty.*

None of these approaches is right or wrong. They can all succeed brilliantly. But someone who's programmed to use one style will feel awkward and discouraged trying to follow another. We can all master each style if we have to, the way a mole can swim or an otter can climb trees, but it's not a best-case scenario.

So I finally stopped pressuring Katie to act like her Follow Thru teachers or her Quick Start mother. Instead I helped her find detailed information and gave her time to absorb it. She recently devoured a 1,000-page book on

Web site design that I would not read if the alternative were death on the rack. It took her a month to finish the book. The next day, she made a Web site. Spooky.

## Play to your strengths

Once you know your instinctive style, brainstorm ways to make it work for you, not against you. For starters, choose fields of endeavor where you feel comfortable and competent. If you love systematic structure, don't become a freelancer. If you are crazy about physical models, don't force yourself to crunch financial statistics for a living.

To really boost your sense of self-efficacy, think of ways you could modify your usual tasks to suit your personal style. For example, Kathy suggested that Katie might ask for permission to do detailed research reports in place of other school assignments. I nearly threw up at the very thought, but to my astonishment Katie agreed enthusiastically.

Of course, you'll inevitably interact with people whose instinctive patterns are different from yours. Otter, Mole, Squirrel, and Mouse may all show up in the same family, workplace, or book club. Occasionally, it's fine to conform, using styles of action that don't come naturally—but do it consciously and for a limited time, or your sense of self-efficacy will suffer. And finally...

## Team up with unlike others

As long as Otter, Mole, Squirrel, and Mouse are forced to race in the same terrain, at least three of them will be out of their element, looking and feeling like failures. But think what they could do if they pooled their skills. They could access resources from the water, earth, trees, and fields, combining them in ways none of the animals could achieve alone. They could rule the world! (Or at least the backyard.)

This is the very best way to leverage an understanding of conative style—to create useful, complementary strategies instead of disheartening, competitive ones. Many of us have spent a lifetime trying to be what we're not, feeling lousy about ourselves when we fail and sometimes even when we succeed. We hide our differences when, by accepting and celebrating them, we could collaborate to make every effort more exciting, productive, enjoyable, and powerful. Personally, I think we should start right now. I mean, hey, how hard can it be?

JANUARY 2006

# Guide to Avoiding Avoidance

........................................................................

*Is there really such a thing as good grief? Does fear of suffering only increase suffering? For the fastest way through bad times, read on....*

........................................................................

elanie's life was shrinking like a cheap blouse in an overheated dryer. At 30 she'd developed a fear of flying that ended her dream of world travel. Within a year, her phobia had grown to include— or rather, exclude—driving. After the World Trade Center attacks, Melanie became terrified to enter the downtown area of any city. She quit her job as an office manager (the potential for mail-based terrorism was too big) and called me hoping I could help her devise a way of earning money from home. "Everybody tells me my fears aren't realistic," she said. "But I think I'm the most realistic person I know. It's a dangerous world—I just want to be safe."

There was only one thing for which Melanie would leave her apartment. Once a month, she walked to a run-down neighborhood to meet her drug dealer, who sold her Xanax and OxyContin of questionable purity. I insisted that Melanie see a psychiatrist before I'd work with her, and the worried shrink called me before the impression of Melanie's posterior had faded from his visitor chair. "She's taking enough medication to kill a moose," he told me. "If she slipped in the shower and knocked herself out, withdrawal could kill her before she regained consciousness."

Ironic, *n'est-ce pas?* Safety-obsessed Melanie was positively devil-may-care when it came to better living through chemistry. This made no sense to me—until I realized that Melanie's objective wasn't really to avoid danger but to prevent the feeling of fear. Melanie was using a strategy psychologist Steven Hayes, PhD, calls experiential avoidance, dodging external experiences in an effort to ward off distressing emotions. It wasn't working. It never does. In fact, to keep her tactics from destroying her, she would have to learn the antidote for experiential avoidance—and so must the rest of us, if we want our lives to grow larger and more interesting, rather than smaller and more disappointing.

## Why Experiential Avoidance Seems Like a Good Idea

Most of us do this kind of emotional side step, at least occasionally. Maybe, like Melanie, you feel skittish on airplanes, so you take the train instead. In the realm of physical objects, dodging situations associated with pain is a wonderfully effective strategy; it keeps us from pawing hot stovetops, swallowing tacks, and so on. Shouldn't the same logic apply to psychological suffering? According to Hayes, it doesn't. Experiential avoidance usually increases the hurt it is meant to eliminate.

Consider Melanie, who, quite understandably, wanted to steer clear of the awful sensation of being afraid. Every time she withdrew from a scary activity, she got a short-term hit of relief. But the calm didn't last. Soon fear would invade the place to which Melanie had retreated—for example, she felt much better driving than flying for a little while, but it wasn't long before she was as petrified in cars as airplanes. Drugs calmed her at first, but soon she became terrified of losing her supply. By the time we met, her determination to bypass anything scary had trapped her in a life completely shaped by fear.

The reason this happens, according to Hayes and other devotees of relational frame theory, is that Melanie's brain works through forming connections and associations. So does yours. Your verbal mind is one big connection generator. Try this: Pick two unrelated objects that happen to be near you. Next answer this question: How are they alike? For instance, if the objects are a book and a shoe, you might say they're alike because they both helped you get a job (by being educated and dressing well). Ta-da! Your book, your shoe, and your job are linked by a new neural connection in your brain. Now you're more likely to think of all these things when you think of any given one.

This means that every time you avoid an event or activity because it's painful, you automatically connect the discomfort with whatever you do instead. Suppose I'm having a terrible hair day, and to not feel that shame, I cancel a meeting with a client. Just thinking about that client brings on a pang of shame. If I watch a movie to distract myself, I may be hit with an unpleasant twinge just hearing the name of that movie. This happens with every form of psychological suffering we try to outrun. When we run from our feelings, they follow us. Everywhere.

## The Willingness Factor

In Hayes's book *Get Out of Your Mind & into Your Life*, he suggests that we picture our minds as electronic gadgets with dials, like old-fashioned radios. One dial is labeled Emotional Suffering (Hayes actually calls it Discomfort). Naturally, we do everything we can to turn that dial to zero. Some people do this all their lives, without ever noticing that it never works. The hard truth is that we have no ultimate control over our own heartaches.

There's another dial on the unit, but it doesn't look very enticing. This one Hayes calls Willingness, though I think of it as Willingness to Suffer. It's safe to assume that we start life with that dial set at zero, and we rarely see any reason to change it. Increasing our availability to pain, we think, is just a recipe for anguish soufflé.

Well, yes...except life, as Melanie so astutely commented, is dangerous. It'll upset you every few minutes or so, sometimes mildly, sometimes apocalyptically. Since desperately twisting down the Emotional Suffering dial only makes things worse, Hayes suggests that we try something radical: Leave that dial alone—abandon all attempts to skirt unpleasant emotions—and focus completely on turning up our Willingness to Suffer.

What this means, in real-world terms, is that we stop avoiding experiences because we're afraid of the unpleasant feelings that might come with them. We don't seek suffering or take pride in it; we just stop letting it dictate any of our choices. People who've been through hell are often forced to learn this, which is why activist, cancer patient, and poet Audre Lorde wrote, "When I dare to be powerful—to use my strength in the service of my vision, then it becomes less and less important whether I am afraid."

Once we're willing to confront our emotional suffering, we begin making choices based on attraction instead of aversion, love instead of fear. Where we used to think about what was "safe," we now become interested in doing what seems right or fun or meaningful or ripe with possibilities. Ask yourself this: What would I do if I stopped try-ing to avoid emotional pain? Think of at least three answers (though 30 would be great and 300 even better).

Stick with this exercise until you get a glimmer of what life without avoidance would be like. To paraphrase Dr. Seuss, Oh, the places you'd go! Oh, the people you'd meet, the food you'd eat, the jokes you'd tell, the clothes you'd wear, the changes you'd spark in the world!

## The Consequences of Willingness

What happens when we're willing to feel bad is that, sure enough, we often feel bad—but without the stress of futile avoidance. Emotional discomfort, when accepted, rises, crests, and falls in a series of waves. Each wave washes parts of us away and deposits treasures we never imagined. No one would call it easy, but the rhythm of emotional pain that we learn to tolerate is natural, constructive, and expansive. It's different from unwilling suffering the way the sting of disinfectant is different from the sting of decay; the pain leaves you healthier than it found you.

It took Melanie a huge leap of faith to accept this. She finally decided to turn up her Willingness to Suffer dial, simply because her Emotional Suffering levels were mani-festly out of her control. She started by joining a yoga class, though the thought of it scared her witless. She found that her anxiety spiked, fluctuated, and gradually declined. Over the ensuing months, she entered therapy, traded her street-drug habit for prescribed medication, and found a new job. Melanie's worry isn't completely gone; it probably never will be. But that doesn't matter much. She is willing to accept discomfort in the pursuit of happiness, and that means she'll never be a slave to fear again.

To the extent that we reject anything we love solely because of what we fear, we're all like Melanie. Find a place in your life where you're practicing experiential avoidance, an absence where you wish there were something wonderful. Then commit to the process of getting it, including any inherent anxiety or sadness. Get on an airplane not because you're convinced it won't crash, but because meeting your baby niece is worth a few hours of terror. Sit on the beach with your mocha latte, humming the song you shared with your ex, and let grief wash through you until your memories are more sweet than bitter. Pursue your dreams not because you're immune to heartbreak but because your real life, your whole life, is worth getting your heart broken a few thousand times.

When fear makes your choices for you, no security measures on earth will keep the things you dread from finding you. But if you can avoid avoidance—if you can choose to embrace experiences out of passion, enthusiasm, and a readiness to feel whatever arises—then nothing, nothing in all this dangerous world, can keep you from being safe.

FEBRUARY 2006

# The Sponge People

*Here's how to protect yourself from inadvertently
taking in other people's stress.*

Virginia is a medical researcher who came to see me in a last-ditch attempt to deal with overwhelming negative emotions that tended to beset her at work. She liked her job, but when she interacted with certain colleagues, she was flooded with anxiety, sadness, indignation and other inexplicable feelings. Virginia was sure those reactions came from her own neuroses, but therapy hadn't fixed the problem. After talking to her for half an hour, I thought I knew why.

"I don't think you're neurotic," I told her. "I think you're spongy." I explained that some people put out a lot of emotional energy—her noxious coworkers, for example—and others pick up a lot of it, like Virginia.

She stared at me as though she'd just noticed crunchy granola spilling from my ears. In her orthodox science worldview, my Theory of Emotional Sponginess was definitely not kosher. But I've seen so many people struggling with the effects of this mysterious phenomenon that I now take it for granted. Not everyone is spongy like Virginia, but those who are can learn to protect themselves from inadvertently taking in other people's stress.

Ever since Emile Durkheim's landmark work *Suicide* appeared in 1897, sociologists have accepted the possibility that self-slaughter can be communicable. So can panic, laughter, hope, violence, financial strategies, and the urge to solve Rubik's Cubes. Behaviors, moods, and fads seem to infect people just like germs, spreading through populations in epidemic waves.

A few researchers have tried to pinpoint the mechanism of contagious psychological phenomena. For example, biologist Rupert Sheldrake, PhD, studies the experience of "telephone telepathy"—knowing who's calling on the phone before you answer it. When subjects were asked to guess which friend or relative was calling them, they were far more accurate than would be expected by chance. When the callers were strangers, though, their guesses were statistically random. Sheldrake concluded that we can sense when people we care about are thinking about us, even at great distances.

We all know this is irrational. How embarrassing, then, that so many of us have had the experience of knowing who's calling the second the phone rings, or even a few seconds before. How unbelievable that my son, who has Down syndrome, regularly talks to me about things I'm thinking, even when I haven't said a word out loud. How ridiculous that so many of my clients, like Virginia, walk away from interpersonal interactions flooded with whatever emotions happen to ride in on the coattails of their associates.

"Humor me," I tell Virginia. "Let's try something. Hold out your arm, parallel to the floor. I'm going to push down on your hand. You resist me. Keep your arm stuck out straight."

Virginia plays along, and I give several experimental pushes. Sometimes as I push, I think, *You're a terrible person!* Sometimes I think, *You're fabulous!* I try to keep the pressure consistent and my face expressionless. Just as I expect, Virginia's arm feels much stronger when I'm thinking positive thoughts about her. When my thoughts are negative, she's as weak as a kitten.

Virginia doesn't like this. She frowns and demands many repeats, just as I did when I learned this homespun experiment from two social-scientist friends. I was stunned at how noodle-like my arm became when my friends thought negative things about me. Since then I've repeated this process with dozens of clients. When speaking to groups, I often choose two volunteers (one pusher, one pushee), who test their strength as everyone else in the room thinks critical or supportive thoughts about the person being pushed. I give the crowd random hand signals—thumbs up for nice vibes, thumbs down for mean ones—that can't be seen by the volunteers. The group's thoughts should not affect the subject's strength. But they almost always do.

Grab some friends and try this experiment yourself. If your group is anything like the ones I've worked with, you or your compadres will find your arm strength varying in response to one another's thoughts. Perhaps one of you will insist that this shift happens because you were communicating subtle cues through facial expression, body language, or some other physical action. Could be true, but whatever the mechanism—telephone telepathy or imperceptible physical signs—the fact is that many people are sitting ducks for social contagion.

If this experiment doesn't affect you—if your arm strength doesn't vary depending on what other people are thinking—feel free to become a repossession officer or divorce lawyer. What the heck, run for president. You'll continually interact with people who dislike you, but it won't bother you a bit.

Shielding yourself from a coworker's or family member's stress or high-pitch negativity requires constructing a suit of psychological armor. Most of my clients, Virginia included, can do this simply by visualizing a situation in which they feel deeply calm. Picturing the best day you spent with your funniest friend or remembering a day at the beach with your dog might be enough protection for you.

Extremely spongy people may have to try a number of visualizations before finding the right defense. Check for effectiveness with the arm test: Ask your friends to come back over; keep holding different positive images in your mind's eye until you find that your arm is able to retain its muscle strength no matter what ugly thoughts others are sending your way. The delightful thing about this kind of safeguard is that it allows nourishing energy to reach you but deflects the stuff that's poisonous.

I wrote a checklist on the back of a business card so that Virginia could read over it in emergency situations and learn to "armor up."

### **A** *is for Acknowledge*

Spongy people who start to feel uneasy in company will often dismiss or tamp down their feelings, but a better idea is to let those emotions loose. Like a spiking fever in an ill patient, the wave of emotion is the beginning of the healing process.

### **R** *is for Recognize*

What, exactly, does the emotion feel like? You may realize that the feeling fits the person next to you better than it does you (you're angry when they've been wronged, anxious when they're stressed out). The mismatch is evidence that a feeling is contagion based.

### **M** *is for Monitor*

Sometimes the difference between your feelings and the other's is hard to describe—a bit like the difference between nutmeg and cinnamon—but you might be able to discern which is which if you track what happens in your psyche before, during, and especially after you've been around specific people. You'll begin to notice patterns—that you're always angry after dinner with one friend or nervous after a day with your high-strung aunt.

### O *is for Observe*

The most powerful tool for emotional detachment is observation. As a highly contagious person gets closer to you, watch the interaction and resulting emotions as if you were a third party—something like "Huh, there's that surge of envy I always get around jealous Marcella." Active observation can help the spongiest person detach.

### R *is for Relax*

If simply noticing the extra sensations rattling around your consciousness isn't enough of a remedy, take a deep breath and exhale completely while relaxing all your muscles. Negative energy will lessen.

### S *is for Space*

The gap between the words *armor* and *up* is a reminder to get real physical distance from emotionally contagious people. Walk into the next room. Take a potty break. If only for a minute, find a little private turf to continue watching your mind, breathing deeply, and relaxing physically.

### **U** *is for Understand*

Few contagious people are deliberately trying to upset others; most are unaware that their anger or frustration or post-work venting can affect more yielding friends and family. Understanding that this is simply the way they're built frees you to tap into your compassion for them. If a stressed-out person wants to inflict her anxiety on you—and she's successful at it—simply realizing that you have methods to block social contagion can help you feel far less susceptible to it.

### **P** *is for Protect*

The last step in the "armor up" process is to return to the mental image (or images) that connects you to the peaceful balance of your core self. Maintain your psychological shield by spending a few minutes a day visualizing this image, say, while you're driving or washing dishes. The idea is to make the image easily accessible, a way of keeping your armor at the ready.

If you're a bit spongy, vulnerable to the unsettling energy of others, count yourself lucky. You've been given an incentive to armor up, to consciously screen out the ubiquitous stresses that afflict humanity. Create your shining suit, keep your checklist on hand, and head out into battle, knowing that the power to keep yourself safe from social contagion is one thing you'll always find within.

JUNE 2006

# How to Deal with the Highly Defensive People in Your Life

"I want your honest opinion," said my friend Joanna, handing me her unpublished manuscript. "Don't whitewash; tell the truth. Promise!"

So I promised—apprehensively. Joanna's very talented, but I know she also takes criticism hard. To my relief, I loved her book, and I fired off an e-mail saying that the only way she could possibly improve it would be to make it a little more personal. "You're so amazing," I told her. "Putting more of you in the book would take it from great to sublime."

Joanna didn't write back for nearly a month. When she did, it was to tell me that my "attack" had left her "inconsolable."

Oy.

I'd made a crucial mistake when I agreed to be Joanna's critic: I ignored my knowledge that she is a highly defensive person. People like her (let's call them HDPs for short) can be found in almost every family, workplace, or crowd. Dealing with them requires a special set of skills, a defense against defensiveness. I recommend keeping these techniques handy for dealing with the HDPs in your life—or for minimizing your own defensiveness, should it ever raise its touchy little head.

## The Dark Side of Sensitivity

Joanna describes herself as sensitive, and she is. But her reaction to my comments wasn't sensitivity; it was defensiveness. The two may feel identical to the person experiencing them, but actually they're worlds apart. Sensitivity is born of careful attention. It involves looking closely, understanding deeply, and therefore not causing harm. Defensiveness, on the other hand, is the bastard child of shame. For people who have survived harshly judgmental environments, shame—the sick sense that they're basically inadequate—dominates the psychological landscape. They're sensitive the way a truckload of TNT is sensitive. Virtually any bump or jostle causes them to explode, often harming others.

Knowing an HDP's destructive behavior comes from shame doesn't excuse it. But at least it helps me understand why one of my clients dumped her boyfriend for "implying she was ugly" because he closed his eyes when they kissed, or why I once saw a party guest respond to the question, "Would you like some wine?" by snapping, "Why, do I look like an alcoholic?" From the outside, defensive behavior is disproportionate, bizarre, often appalling. But from the perspective of the HDPs, these actions are justifiable—no, necessary!—self-protection. I've spent a long time thinking about the best way to deal effectively with such people.

## How to Have a Functional, Trusting, Relaxed, Mutually Satisfying Human Relationship with a Highly Defensive Person

Short answer: You can't.

Long answer: You really can't. Don't even try.

The reason one can't look to defensive people for top-quality relationships is that such relationships require two human beings. But defensive people don't think like humans. They think like reptiles. I mean this literally. Beneath the elaborate neural structures that mediate our subtle social interactions, we all possess what scientists call a reptilian brain. This ancient biological structure, which evolved in reptiles, isn't capable of nuanced emotion or logical thought. Its primary driving force is fear. Two fears, to be specific.

The first worry of all reptile brains (including yours and mine) is "I don't have enough!" Not enough love, money, food, credit, glory—the subject of our deprivation obsessions varies, but the theme "not enough" pounds away like a monotonous drumbeat. The only thing as loud to the reptile ear is its other major concern: "Someone's out to get me!" An HDP perceives threat coming from lots of sources; one day the Enemy may be a coworker, the next a relative, the next an entire nation. But to the reptile brain, someone, somewhere, is always about to attack.

This makes evolutionary sense. Lizards live longer if they obsessively acquire more food, shelter, and mates, and if they expect predators to jump them at any moment. Sadly, however, reptiles are blind to nondefensive emotions; to the glow of love, the tickle of amusement. The only thing playing on their mental screens, all day every day, is The Lack and Attack Show. The same is true of HDPs. When humans are gripped by primal fear, they become their inner lizards—and HDPs are virtually always gripped by primal fear.

So the best relationship you can hope to sustain with a defensive person is the sort you might have with a reptile. As a doctor here in Arizona once explained to a man who was bitten on the lip while kissing his pet rattlesnake (it made the newspapers), you simply cannot expect a loving connection from a reptile, even if you raised it from the egg. Remembering that these people are basically giant talking lizards will keep you from futilely trying to please them, persuade them, or explain yourself to them. That's a key step. But a solid defense against defensiveness requires you to go further—to manage the fear that may put you in HDP mode.

## How to Avoid Becoming a Highly Defensive Person

Defensiveness is extremely contagious. When Joanna "forgave" me for what I thought was glowingly positive feedback, I felt a jolt of angry defensiveness myself. If I'd followed my own inner lizard, with its worries of being insufficiently loved and excessively criticized, I'd have accused Joanna of being paranoid—which would've sent her inner lizard into all-out combat mode, triggering still more defensiveness in me, resulting in a relationship catastrophe I call War of the Dinosaurs (dinosaur means "fearfully great lizard").

It's easy to say that we should stay out of reptile mode, but that's hard advice to follow when some HDP launches an attack—especially if the person has any power over you. When your highly defensive parent, boss, head nurse, or gang leader launches a dinosaur attack, you may not be able to stop yourself from getting upset in return. But if you can't help slithering into reptile mode, there's still one option left: Don't go lizard. Go turtle.

### The Shell Game

One reason the Roman Empire conquered most of ancient Europe was a military maneuver called the turtle. In battles a regiment would clump together, the soldiers in the center holding their shields above their heads, while those on the periphery shielded the unit's front, back, and sides. They'd march along that way, pretty much an indestructible human tortoise. You, too, need such tactics for engaging with HDPs who loom above you in the social-power landscape.

"Going turtle" means putting up an emotional shell. This isn't easy, because mirror neurons in your brain fire in resonance with the feelings of people around you. If you and I were talking, part of your brain would organize itself to match part of mine, and vice versa. When you're with a loving person, this is wonderful; with an HDP, it creates wars straight out of the Mesozoic era. To avoid conflagration, you must pull your sensitive social neurons back into a shell.

It isn't all that hard. Try this: Think about an occasion when an HDP blew up at you. Remember the shock, the anger, the urge to lash back. Got it? Good. Now picture your living room painted kumquat orange. Then figure out whether 713 is a prime number. Do you notice how your mind lets go of emotional reactivity as it attacks visual or analytical problems? Artists and scientists are notoriously eccentric because their mental work diverts brainpower from social connection. When I'm listening to an HDP's rant, I am also, almost always, thinking about painting. Desert landscapes, usually. They help my inner turtle feel safe, so that I don't mirror the aggression of the HDP.

## Next Step: The High Road

Pulling into an emotional shell is better than engaging in dinosaur warfare, and can allow you to converse with HDPs without being destroyed. An even higher goal than turtling, however, is to remain fearlessly human in the face of hostility. My idol, in this regard, is dear departed Steve Irwin, the crocodile hunter, who loved reptiles unabashedly and unilaterally, even as he grappled and sidestepped to avoid their violent attacks. There are many HDPs in my life I really enjoy, the way Steve Irwin enjoyed his crocs. Joanna, for example, is a good friend and wonderful writer, especially for a lizard.

You can learn a lot about handling HDPs by studying the way Irwin treated his beloved reptiles: firmly but lovingly. "You're all right, sweetheart," he'd croon as a sea snake tried desperately to envenomate him. "Aren't you gorgeous!" he'd exult to a charging one-eyed alligator. And you could tell he meant it. I think HDPs all over the world must have felt strangely happy watching Steve lovingly disarm reptiles like themselves.

If you're feeling brave enough, try the crocodile hunter's techniques on a highly defensive person. See something beautiful in them, and steadfastly mirror that instead of their antagonism. I've used the above Irwinisms—"You're all right, sweetheart" and "Aren't you gorgeous!"—and found them very effective, even in business negotiations. But my favorite reptile-wrangling skill, the one I used with Joanna, consists of three ridiculously simple words: "All is well."

Try saying this, warmly, the next time an HDP lashes out at you. "You attacked my writing!" All is well. "You're implying I'm ugly!" All is well. "Do I look like an alcoholic to you?" All is well. It may sound off-point, but since extreme defensiveness is itself off-point, this actually works better than following your HDP's arguments. When I assured Joanna, "All is well," she instantly relaxed. Keeping "All is well" on the tip of your tongue can disarm bullies, mend marriages, stop fistfights. It's a three-word de-defensivizer.

Say it now, to feel it in your mouth and mind. Repeat the whole classic mantra: "All is well, and all will be well, and all manner of things will be well." Feel how this soothes your inner lizard. It works so well I don't even care if it's true—though I suspect it may be, in some mystical realm that mortal eyes see only through a glass, darkly. But one thing's for sure, even in the workaday world, where friends may turn into dinosaurs and you're stuck with an exploding coworker: If you have a few reptile-wrangling tricks under your belt, all will be a heck of a lot better.

MAY 2007

# The Anti-Complain Campaign

a t 63, Minnie is one of the youngest people I've ever met. She sparkles, and not just because she's dressed in a fabulous buttercup-yellow tank top bedecked with rhinestones and sequins. Everything about Minnie, from her laughter to the successful businesses she's created, seems to shine.

This radiance didn't come easily. Minnie was once a young widow, grieving the death of her husband and one of her two children. When I ask how she rose from this desolation to her success as a mother and a professional, Minnie thinks for a minute, then says, "I just got tired of hearing myself whine. I harnessed my complaining energy and used it to create a really good life."

This isn't the first time I've heard such a story. While many people spend whole lifetimes complaining, most of the high achievers I know divert the energy of frustration away from complaint and into success. I've tried both paths. I can enjoy a good whine the way connoisseurs enjoy a good wine, but eventually, like Minnie, I get sick of my own petulance. Then I embark on something you might want to try: a "venting fast." It's not for the fainthearted, but it's a powerful way to create a better life.

### What's a venting fast?

On the surface, it's a simple thing. Here are the instructions:

1. *For a period of time, say a week or a month, stop complaining aloud about anything, to anybody.*

2. *When the urge to fuss arises, vent on paper. Start with the words "I'm upset about." Then describe whatever's bothering you.*

3. *Think of at least one thing you can do to actually change the frustrating situation. Write it down.*

4. *If you can't think of any positive action steps, simply continue to resist venting out loud. Eventually, your frustration will increase until you think, "I'm so upset I just want to…" Write down what you want to do.*

> 5. Do it. Divorce the guy, cuss in front of your
> fundamentalist sister, put off lunching with the
> passive-aggressive "friend" until the end of time.

If you think that a venting fast requires willpower, you're half right. After a few whine-free days, you'll find that it also requires courage—possibly more than you've ever used. To understand why anyone would put themselves through a venting fast, it helps to know a little about the psychological dynamics of complaint.

Complaining is as useful for people's minds as a whistle vent is for a teakettle. We use the phrase "let off steam" because frustration affects our behavior the way heat affects liquid in a container. As the level of negative emotion rises, we feel mounting pressure. We can handle this pressure in the same three ways we can handle steam:

## Option 1: Explosion

Many people try to deal with the hot vapor of irritation by simply choking it back. This leads to behavioral explosions, as you can learn from anyone who's ever tried to be the perfect, unruffled mother, only to find herself locked in the bathroom punching towels and using language that would make pirates faint.

Or maybe that's just me.

So here's another example: The nursing staff at an inner-city hospital once told me that although treating drug addicts and gunshot victims was a scary proposition, the most ter-rifying thing they ever had to face (no offense—I'm just repeating what I was told) was a partially anesthetized nun. Dramatic things happened, the nurses averred, when a holy sister from the neighborhood convent was "going under," drugged just beyond inhibition but not yet to oblivion. The nurses told tales of physical violence, of naked escapes from the OR, of destructive rampages through other patients' rooms—all perpetrated by brave, godly women who in their right minds never vented about anything.

Apparently, even those of us with the awesome self-control of religious renunciants occasionally need to release psychological pressure. You wouldn't want to emerge from an appendectomy to discover that you've decked the entire surgical team with your own IV rack, would you? That's where a strategy of controlled release comes in.

### Option 2: Venting

The effect of emotional venting is to sustain an unsat-isfactory status quo. Most people think the opposite, that complaining is part of an effort to change an unsatisfying situation. Nope. Complaining lets off pressure so that we neither explode with frustration nor feel compelled to take the often risky steps of openly opposing a difficult person or situation. Keeping emotional pressure tolerably low doesn't change problematic circumstances but rather perpetuates them.

For instance, Regina is a Mexican-American whose white racist parents-in-law treated her abominably. She complained about this to her husband every day. When I asked why she talked to her husband, she said she was starting an information chain: She would force him to force his parents to change. How long had Regina been employing this strategy? Twenty years. And the effect to date? Nada.

Mike worked for a pompous boss who gave his subordinates little direction and less support. The underlings spent their work hours muttering angry stories and following the soap opera of office conflict. Mike came home exhausted, not from working but from venting. And things at work kept getting worse, not better.

College sophomore Dinah spent hours with her friends ranting about a certain high-ranking elected official, who shall remain nameless. This, Dinah told me, was activism. I said it looked more like passivism—neither activism nor pacifism but an excellent way of feeling intelligent and important without studying.

These venters thought their chronic complaining was "powerful civil disobedience." Actually, it was disempowering uncivil obedience. By allowing emotional pressure to dissipate without action, these people were able to sit indefinitely in predicaments that pushed them to an emotional boiling point. Now, in situations you don't want to change, this can be a good idea. I was a better mother to my toddlers after a session of recreational complaining with other moms. Having vented about our sleep deprivation, boredom, and longing for adult company, we'd return to the field of battle—er, motherhood—able to focus on the sweeter aspects of parenting. In Minnie's case, venting helped ease the anguish of losing loved ones. Without it, she might not have survived her grief. But even she reached the point where venting felt excessive, like an illness rather than a cure. Then it was time for Option 3: creating a steam-driven life.

## Option 3: Harnessing the Power of Frustration

"It is not that I do not get angry," said Gandhi. "I do not give vent to anger." On another occasion he wrote, "As heat conserved is transmuted into energy, even so our anger controlled can be transmuted into a power which can move the world." Gandhi was describing the power of a mind that refuses to vent frustration, channeling it into productive action the way an engine harnesses steam heat.

If you want to know how much change this can cause, consider the millennia that humans spent watching vapor rise from their cook pots before a 17th-century genius thought, "Hey, I think all that steam could drive a piston." *Et voilà*: the Industrial Revolution. A mere 200 years later, people were walking on the moon. This is the level of transformation that can occur when we stop complaining about our circumstances and begin channeling our emotional pressure into positive action. Look how Gandhi changed the world. He was one of the great peacemakers in all history! Right up until someone shot him!

Oh, yeah. That.

Make no mistake, a venting fast is risky. Without the option of complaining, you'll have only two choices for dealing with emotional buildup: explosion or positive action. The first will damage you, your relationships, your life. The second will fundamentally alter the status quo, and the status quo, by definition, resists change. If you follow the venting-fast rules above, you're almost certain to break implicit or explicit social rules that now govern your life. Prepare to find this terrifying.

When Regina stopped complaining about her in-laws, her emotional steam pressure quickly rendered her unable to tolerate their company. One day, when her father-in-law made a racist comment, Regina stood up and took a cab home. "I was terrified," she told me later. "But I had to do something." The ensuing argument between Regina's husband and his parents was the beginning of overdue but impressive change. Faced with the choice of being respectful or losing their son, the bigots began showing respect.

Mike's story was simpler. When he stopped complaining at the office, he became so sick of his boss and bored with his co-workers' venting that he sought, and found, a job he liked better. The end.

Dinah stopped joining in college vent-fests, but her political discontent continued. She'd always been a mediocre student, but the energy she'd been pouring into complaint now drove her to study political science. Diligently. Dinah is now in law school, thinking up ways to create a just society, rather than simply criticizing the people in power. When she runs for office, I'm voting for her.

If you try a venting fast and survive, you may find yourself heading in new, exciting directions. You may even decide to do what Minnie did: commit to an entire life without complaining. "I have a rule," says Minnie, smile and sequins flashing. "I'm not allowed to whine about anything I can change. And since I can always change my attitude, I don't expect to find a really hopeless situation in this lifetime."

I admire this position enormously, though I don't think I'm quite ready to emulate it. Recreational complaining, the sense of steam leaving those emotional vents, is still perversely enjoyable for me. Maybe someday I'll be like Minnie, who's more vibrant and successful in her seventh decade than most people are in their third. Maybe I'll go on a venting fast that lasts the rest of my life. Until then, my existence will fail to match its potential. But I'm not complaining.

At least that's a start.

OCTOBER 2007

# Escape Your Rat Race

*Feeling trapped by a job, relationship, or routine, but terrified of making a change? Feel your way to freedom.*

Sheila and I are conversing at a drug treatment center, where she's been remanded. Counselors are listening, so we can't plan a way to break her out. As it happens, escape is the last thing on Sheila's mind. I'm not coaching her through the woes of being institutionalized for drug use but prepping her for her upcoming release.

"In here everything's simple," Sheila says. "Outside I'll have to deal with my crazy mom, get a job, pay the bills. I don't know how to handle that without drugs." When I ask her to picture a peaceful, happy life, Sheila draws a blank. "I can't imagine anything except what I've already seen," she says.

The despair in her voice is so heavy it makes me want to huff a little glue myself, but two things give me hope: a fabled land known in the annals of psychology as Rat Park, and a montage of other clients, once as hopeless as Sheila, who went on to live happy, meaningful lives. The concepts I learned from Rat Park, channeled through the behaviors I've seen in those courageous clients, just may transform Sheila's future.

But first, what is this mythic Rat Park? And how might it relate to you? The term comes from a study conducted in 1981 by psychologist Bruce Alexander and colleagues. He noted that many addiction studies had something in common: The lab rats they used were locked in uncomfortable, isolating cages. Testing a hunch, Alexander gathered two groups of rats. For the first, he built a 200-square-foot rodent paradise called Rat Park. There a colony of white Wister rats found luxurious accommodations for all their favorite pastimes—mingling, mating, raising pups, writing articles for newspaper tabloids. The second group was housed in the traditional cages.

Alexander offered both groups a choice of plain water or sugar water laced with morphine. Like rats in other studies, the traditionally caged animals became instant addicts. However, the residents of Rat Park tended to "just say no," avoiding the drug-treated sugar water. Even rats that were already addicted to morphine tended to lay off the hard stuff when in Rat Park. Put them back in their cages, however, and they'd stay stoned as Deadheads.

Alexander saw many parallels between these junkie rats and human addicts. He has talked of one patient who worked as a shopping mall Santa. "He couldn't do his job unless he was high on heroin," Alexander remembered. "He would shoot up, climb into that red Santa Claus costume, put on those black plastic boots, and smile for six hours straight."

This story jingles bells for many of my clients. Like Smack Santa, they spend many hours playing roles that don't match their innate personalities and preferences, dulling the pain with mood-altering substances. Miserable with their jobs, relationships, or daily routines, they gulp down a fifth of Scotch, buy 46 commemorative Elvis plates on QVC, superglue phony smiles to their faces, and head on out to whatever rat race is gradually destroying them.

Sheila was actually a step ahead of most of my clients, in that she knew she was locked up. Most people are trapped in prisons made of mind stuff—attitudes and beliefs such as "I have to look successful" or "I can't disappoint my dad." Ideas like these—being deeply entrenched and invisible— are often more powerful than physical prisons. When we're trapped in mind cages, gulping happy pills by the handful, and fantasizing about lethally stapling coworkers, we rarely even consider that our unhappiness comes from living in captivity. And if we ever come close to recognizing the truth, we're stopped by a barrage of terrifying questions: "What if there's nothing better than this?" "What if I quit my job, lose my seniority, and end up somewhere even worse?" "What if I break off this relationship and end up alone forever?" "What if I get my hopes up and the big break never comes?"

When the alternatives are staying in the familiar cage or facing the unknown, trust me, most people choose the cage—over and over and over again. It's painful to watch, especially knowing that liberation is only a few simple steps away. If you suspect that you might need to engineer your own prison break, the following pieces of commonsense advice can set you free forever.

### You Don't Have to Know What Rat Park Looks Like

"I just don't think I'll ever find the right life for me," Sheila frets.

"Of course you won't!" I say. "How strange to think you would!"

It amazes me how often people use that phrase: "Find the right life." Would you walk into your kitchen hoping to find the right fried egg, the right cup of coffee, the right toast? Such things don't simply appear before you; they arrive because you rummage around, figure out what's available, and make what you want. (If you're rich, you can hire a chef and place your order, but you're still creating the result.)

Bruce Alexander's rats were hand-delivered into paradise. Lucky critters, indeed—but not nearly as lucky as Alexander himself, or the rest of us humans, who have the astonishing ability to envision and build Rat Parks. All animals are shaped by their environment, but we, more than any other species, can shape our environment right back. We can cook the egg, brew the coffee, paint the room, change the space. We can fabricate our Rat Parks, and we must, if we want them built to spec.

"But I don't know what I'm trying to build," Sheila protests when I tell her this. "How can I create something when I don't have a clue what it looks like?"

Time for commonsense suggestion number two.

## You Don't Need a Map
## to Find Your Rat Park

I often invite clients to play the dead-simple game You're Getting Warmer, You're Getting Colder. The client leaves the room, and I hide a simple object—say, a key—in a tricky place, such as the inside of a cake. (Not that I would have done this with someone locked up. Like Sheila. Absolutely not.) When the client returns to the room, he almost invariably stands still, and asks, "What am I looking for?"

Obviously, I don't answer him. The only feedback I'll give is "You're getting warmer" or "You're getting colder." Eventually clients will start moving. Guided by the words warmer and colder, they quickly identify the general hiding area. Then there's a period of confusion, fueled by assumptions like "Well, she certainly wouldn't hide it in the cake." They go back and forth for a bit, then stop and demand,

"Where is it?" Again, this gets them nothing. Peeved, they revert to following the "warmer/colder" feedback until they arrive at the object.

I've never had a client who didn't ultimately succeed. Not one.

My point: Life has installed within you powerful "getting warmer, getting colder" signals. When Sheila thought of leaving the treatment center, her tension, anxiety, and drug cravings soared. The time she had to serve was "warmer"; her outside life, "colder." Certain activities were freezing cold—dealing with her mother, working, paying bills. As we examined each of these, we found that her guidance system was giving her beautifully clear messages. For instance, being around sane non-criminals, even officials at the treatment center, felt "warmer" than Sheila's crazy dope-dealing mother. Working in the cafeteria, with its institutional predictability, was "warmer" than her old cocktail waitress job, where she'd flashed her flesh to elicit unpredictable tips from drunken customers. Living within her economic means felt "warmer" than credit card shopping sprees she couldn't afford.

True, Sheila was a long way from her own Rat Park. But with the knowledge that her navigation system was functioning perfectly, all she had to do was play her life as a game of You're Getting Warmer, You're Getting Colder. The same is true for you. It isn't necessary to know exactly how your ideal life will look; you only have to know what feels better and what feels worse. If something feels both good and bad, break it down into its components to see which are warm, which cold. Begin making choices based on what makes you feel freer and happier, rather than how you think an ideal life should look. It's the process of feeling our way toward happiness, not the realization of some Platonic ideal that creates our best lives.

"My life is so far from perfect," Sheila says as we end our session. "I don't know if it's fixable."

She's ready to hear my third and last piece of common-sense advice.

## You Don't Have to Make Big Changes to Get There

This step is something I stole from philosopher and engineer Buckminster Fuller. Bucky, as his friends knew him, chose for his epitaph just three words: call me trimtab. Trim tabs are tiny rudders attached to the back of larger rudders that steer huge ships. The big rudders would snap off if turned directly, but, as Fuller famously said, "just moving the little trim tab builds a low pressure that pulls the rudder around. Takes almost no effort at all. So...you can just put your foot out like that and the whole big ship of state is going to go."

Every life is a series of trim-tab decisions. Should you read tonight or watch TV? Choose what feels warmer. Self-help or thriller? Choose what feels warmer. Cuddle with the dog or banish him from the bed? Choose what feels (psychologically) warmer.

If you make mistakes, no problem; you'll soon feel colder and correct your course. Making consistent trim-tab choices toward happiness is what steers the mighty ship of your life into exotic ports, safe havens—in short, into every Rat Park you can imagine, and then some.

I say goodbye to Sheila not knowing whether she'll set her trim tabs toward happiness or back to her drug-abusing cage of a life. I've learned not to get my hopes up with humans, who aren't nearly as clear-sighted and authentic as rats. But our session reminds me to keep following my own tiny feelings and impulses to their distant and amazing destinations. So instead of worrying about Sheila—or me, or you—I'll choose to trust our powerful instincts, our desire to be happy, our amazing human capacity for invention. You may choose cynical despair instead—it's all the rage in intellectual circles—but if you care to join me, I think you'll find it's a whole lot warmer over here in Rat Park.

JANUARY 2009

# When Your Biggest Problem Is . . . You

*Are you driving yourself crazy with dumb mistakes,
"what was I thinking?" comments, and other
lunkheaded moves? Here is a no-fail strategy
to get you back on the right track.*

t's not like I'm shooting myself in the foot," said Whitney. "It's more like I'm using my entire body for target practice. With guns in both hands."

Whitney's problems began when economic chaos hit the advertising company where she was an editor. As Whitney cut redundant prose from ad copy, her company cut redundant workers all around her. Whitney herself had always been a perfectionist who loved her work, but after the downsizing, her performance nose-dived. She began to forget meetings, sleep past her alarm, accidentally forward highly personal e-mails to her boss. On the day she absent-mindedly shredded a presentation she was about to deliver, Whitney came to see me.

"Do I have early-onset Alzheimer's?" she asked desperately. "Maybe ADD? A brain tumor? It's got to be something medical."

Meanwhile, another client of mine—I'll call her Olga—was going through something similar in her relationship with her husband. "Jack is my life," she told me. "I couldn't go on without him." Yet Olga made as many stupid mistakes at home as Whitney did at work. "I forget I've promised to pick him up after work," she told me. "When he says he needs space, I follow him around begging him to talk, and when he wants to be close, I shut down. What's wrong with me?"

Maybe you've had an experience akin to these, a truck-with-no-brakes run of errors and foul-ups that wreak destruction in your life despite frantic efforts to regain control. In the midst of such madness, it can help immensely to know that there's a name for your pain. You may be using something psychologists call a counterphobic mechanism, a tendency to slide toward, not away from, something you fear. Those of us who use plain English might call it self-sabotage—and it can ruin your life. As counterintuitive as it might seem, these subconscious reflexes can be helpful. In these officially Troubled Times, it behooves us all to be aware of them and use them consciously and skillfully.

## Anticipation, Anticipation Is Making Me Late...

"One of my theories," says the evil Count in William Goldman's classic story *The Princess Bride*, "is that pain involves anticipation." He then leaves the captive hero, Westley, chained next to the Machine, a torture device the Count has promised to use on Westley later. An albino dungeon-keeper offers Westley a way out. "You deserve better than what's coming," he says in a moment of compassion. "Please let me kill you. You'll thank me, I swear." Only Westley's superhuman fortitude keeps him from accepting.

The Count's theory about anticipation is right on the money. And self-sabotage is the mind's way of accepting the albino's offer. Like Whitney or Olga, we may screw up in precisely the places we want most to succeed, not realizing that we're subconsciously trying to force a resolution, to stop the anxious feeling that's hanging over our heads, to lose the job rather than continue to worry about a pink slip. To resolve the situation, we must first recognize that we're using counterphobic mechanisms. And that means punching through denial.

### Denial Strategy #1
### "Fear? Ha! What Fear?"

When I suggested to Whitney that she might be courting job loss precisely because it was her worst fear, she laughed.

"Fear? Me? No, absolutely not," she said. "I mean, I'm sorry so many people are getting laid off, but my job is safe as houses."

This struck me as an odd choice of idiom in an era when demented mortgage practices have triggered worldwide economic catastrophe. I also noticed a crimson blush creeping up Whitney's neck. Paging Dr. Freud: Dr. Freud to the floor, please.

"What if you keep shredding presentations and sending your boss e-mails about yeast infections?" I said. "What if these screwups keep getting worse?"

The blush faded abruptly; now Whitney looked pale. "Honestly, I don't see how that's possible," she muttered. "Um, could you excuse me for a second?" She pulled out her BlackBerry and peered at it anxiously.

"You seem nervous," I commented, watching her thumbs go to work.

"Well, of course I'm nervous!" Whitney snapped. "The whole damn country's falling apart—who isn't nervous?"

"So," I said, "suppose your company folds. What would you do?"

"That won't happen."

"I'm not saying it will; I'm just asking you to imagine it."

"I don't want to!"

"Seriously, what will you do if you lose your job?"

The dam burst.

"I've worked my whole adult life for this job!" Whitney cried. "And it's not like I can get another one these days.

Have you seen the news? Every day it's worse—more unemployment, more foreclosures. People just like me are living in tents! My stocks are practically worthless." Whitney began trembling. "I can't lose my job," she whispered. "It'd be the end of the world."

So that cat was out of the bag. Like so many people right now, Whitney was stuck contemplating the Machine of unemployment. But she'd shoved this intense fear out of her conscious awareness, so her subconscious mind had built a counterphobic mechanism to kill the job and end the agony. "You'll thank me," her inner albino was saying. "I swear."

## Denial Strategy #2
### "But That's the Last Thing I'd Want."

For Olga, the problem wasn't that she was unaware of her biggest fear. Quite the contrary. She couldn't answer a telemarketer's call without blurting out her dread of losing Jack. She discussed it endlessly with Jack himself.

"I won't let him talk about anything negative—negative feelings, bad experiences in the past, even movies he doesn't like," she said. "I love him so much; I can't let negative energy into our relationship"

Of course, this bizarre practice ensured that Olga's marriage was focused entirely on negative energy (our lives tend to revolve around the things we're trying not to do). It also meant Jack had no way of processing the countless indignities Olga kept inflicting on him.

"You do understand you're making Jack's life completely impossible?" I said, with my patented anti-tact.

"I know!" Olga said, sobbing. "It's another thing I've done to drive him away, but I can't live without him!"

"So what'll you do if he leaves?"

More sobs. "I don't know; I've never dared think about it."

"If you don't think about it, you're going to have to live through it," I said. "So start thinking."

"Well," she sniffed, "I'd have to learn to live for myself, I guess. I'd have to be independent, to be..." Her voice trailed off, and her mascara-smeared eyes opened wide. "I'd be free," she said.

Whoa, Nelly! The fear she'd been hiding was an even bigger surprise to Olga than Whitney's was to her. Olga's real fear wasn't that Jack wanted to leave her. It was that she wanted to leave Jack.

You may find my treatment of Whitney and Olga rather brutal, but I am not the evil Count. When you're chained to a Machine, though, waiting for God knows what, you have only two options. One is to let the albino dungeon-keeper of your subconscious kill the very thing you fear losing. The other is what brave Westley chose: Face and embrace your fear.

If you're repeatedly making dreadful mistakes and finding yourself in embarrassing snafus in an important area of life, push yourself to contemplate your worst-case scenario.

I suggest doing this in the company of friends, family members, therapists, coaches, or all of the above. While you're gaping and reeling like a stunned mullet, your more objective advisers can help you do some contingency planning. That is what I did with Whitney.

"I know losing your job sounds like the end of the world," I told her. "But it wouldn't be. I know people who've started Internet-based companies for freelance work. They're making more money now than before they were laid off."

"Really?" Whitney blinked. Her grip on the BlackBerry loosened.

"And you'd finally have time to write your own book—haven't you always wanted that?"

"Yes, but how would I—"

"You'd figure it out," I said, hoping like hell I was right.

"You know, I would," said Whitney. She didn't sound totally convinced, not by any means. But she did sound a tiny bit hopeful. Her fear of the Machine was already waning—and that, I knew, would end her unconsciously driven train wrecks at the office. The more we examined ways Whitney could survive being unemployed, the less likely she was to cause that very fate.

Once Olga copped to her real fears, facing and embracing her worst-case scenario was even more liberating. She had felt stifled in her relationship, she realized. Her definition of "perfect wife" had meant someone who relinquished all personal interests except her husband. Although Olga loved Jack, that image of wifehood (hers, not his) was so noxious that subconsciously she knew she couldn't sustain it. Some part of her worried that it would eventually implode. So she'd begun doing things to end the marriage—and thus her terrible anticipation of its end.

As we discussed what Olga might do if she were single, she began redefining herself as an individual, not an appendage. With Jack's help, she bagged her old stereotype of married life and realized she was free to plot her own course. Embracing her worst-case scenario took the kill me now sign off her relationship, and her marriage-torpedoing behaviors stopped.

Since you, like Whitney and Olga, are probably of sound mind, any chronic blundering on your part is likely a counterphobic mechanism: a brave, unconscious, totally knob-brained attempt to end the torture of anticipating further torture. These days, more than ever, facing and embracing your worst-case scenarios, seeing them as problems to be solved rather than torments to suffer helplessly, can save you no end of self-sabotage.

Ironically, of course, this, too, is a counterphobic mechanism. The difference is that it's conscious, reasoned, and wise, rather than unconscious, irrational, and nuts. It may not be fun to contemplate everything that could go wrong in your life, especially in a time of massive economic upheaval and uncertainty. But by going straight into the fear, you can save yourself a crazy go-round with unconscious self-sabotage. You deserve better than that. You'll thank me. I swear.

# How to Tap Into Your True Power

*If you think you have no control over your life, think again. As hemmed in as you may feel, here's how to break out of that helpless place.*

•

'm terrified about my daughter's drinking," Mindy told me during our first session, "but I've asked her to get help, and she just yells at me."

"My boss can be really unethical," said Denise, another client, "but that's the way things work. If I complain, my job is history."

Paula, a third client, is perpetually exhausted: "I know I should take better care of myself," she admitted, "but someone has to be there for my husband and children."

You probably hear statements like these all the time. If you're anything like me, you may make plenty of them yourself. They may not sound dangerous, but they are. They're declarations of powerlessness, one of the most psychologically debilitating conditions human beings can experience. If we believe them, such statements can get us stuck in emotional tar pits ranging from frustration to rage to utter despair. The good news? They're never true.

Never.

I'm not saying we have power over everything in our lives—if that were true, my hair would look so, so different—but I am saying that there's no circumstance in which we are completely powerless. My clients—Mindy, Denise, and Paula—are all being challenged to find their power in a disempowering environment. And whatever your circumstance, so are you.

## Allow the Power

The most common reason we stumble into the delusion of powerlessness is that we're afraid of what other people would do or say or feel if we were to act as we wanted. Mindy was terrified of her daughter's angry resistance. Denise's fear of being fired overrode her ethics. And Paula anxiously predicted that her family would disintegrate if she focused less care on them and more on herself. All three felt stymied, but actually they were just "allower-less" (say it out loud: it rhymes). They were waiting for other people and the arrival of circumstances to give them explicit permission to do what felt right, and by doing so, they were rendering themselves powerless.

I sympathize with my clients' plight, but I wasn't impressed by their claims of powerlessness. I've met too many people who have faced far more daunting circumstances yet refused to be disempowered. For example, my friend and fellow life coach Judy Klipin is a polite little slip of a thing, hardly someone you'd expect to challenge an evil empire.

I'd known Judy for months before she told me about a morning years ago when several police officers barged into her bedroom at 5 A.M. They were seeking evidence of anti-apartheid activity—and it was there. Sitting in plain sight on Judy's nightstand lay a map to the antiapartheid meeting she'd helped organize. Weirdly, the South African police missed this damning document, but they detained Judy anyway, taking her to the infamous headquarters at John Vorster Square, where many activists were held for long periods of time.

"Didn't you feel awfully powerless?" I asked Judy when she told me the story.

"No," she replied, "though I wasn't thrilled when they encouraged me to picture being raped in prison. But as a white university student, I felt relatively safe. Besides, that's not what was important."

What was important, at least to Judy, was resisting an immoral system. For hours, the police tried to break her.

They failed. The only person in police headquarters interested in allowing Judy to follow her moral compass was Judy. But that was enough.

"I was quite cheeky with them," she remembered. "When they asked if I supported Nelson Mandela, I said, 'How would I know? I've never been given an opportunity to hear anything the man has to say!'"

"Had you always stood up for yourself?" I asked.

"Actually, no. I don't know where that behavior came from. I suppose I felt I was protected—not physically, but in a spiritual sense. My parents had always been such strong advocates of equality, as was my childminder, Annie. My first memories are of falling asleep on Annie's back while she sang to me in Setswana. So I'd been raised by three people who were walking testaments that apartheid was insanely wrong. I suppose that gave me permission to stand up for what I believed, no matter what. And because I felt so grounded in that basic sanity, I actually knew that the police were more frightened and powerless than I."

This statement defies all reason—one 95-pound teenage girl more powerful than armed agents of a violent racist regime? But to paraphrase Pascal, there is a reason that reason does not know, and Judy had tapped into that. The way we can allow ourselves to do what we need to, no matter what others may say or do, is to choose love and defy fear.

This has been said so often that I wouldn't even bother mentioning it, except that most of us still don't do it. Want evidence? Go to YouTube, and watch "Linda Hamilton—

What Would You Do?" You'll see an experiment created by a TV news team to test whether ordinary citizens will come to the aid of a needy individual. An actor pretends to faint on a city street while a hidden camera films the scene. In one case, more than 80 people ignore the "injured" actor before someone stops to help. Is the Good Samaritan a wealthy philanthropist? A priest? A doctor? Nope. It's a homeless woman with a gimpy leg. On the video, shot in Newark, New Jersey, you can practically see this "powerless" person connecting with innate compassion, deciding to act, and refusing to give up even when dozens of people ignore her requests to call 911 on their cell phones. She gets creative, calling the unconscious man Billy, humanizing him for others. Eventually, she persuades people to offer assistance. Her name is Linda Hamilton, and she is powerful.

Compare Linda to Mindy, who almost gave up on her belligerent alcoholic daughter—not out of love but because she feared her daughter's anger. Denise said she loved her job, but she had become a lawyer to avoid looking like a "nobody" and supported her unethical boss due to the same fear. The fears that drove Paula's "loving" acts for her family stemmed from fear of being an imperfect homemaker. If you need to distinguish between acts of fear and the power of love, here's a quick guide:

| FEAR | LOVE |
|:---:|:---:|
| *Always feels bad* | *Always feels good* |
| *Motivates grasping* | *Motivates liberation* |
| *Seizes control* | *Relaxes control* |
| *Insists on certainty* | *Accepts uncertainty* |
| *Needs everything* | *Needs nothing* |

The process of spotting fear and refusing to obey it is the source of all true empowerment. Judy did this by choosing beliefs her government called wrong. Linda did it by choosing behavior most passersby saw as foolishly virtuous. Both were bucking social trends, both refused to be scared out of love, and both ultimately prevailed. That's power.

## The Radical Power of Pure Love

This seems a fitting day for me to be writing about powerlessness. It's my son Adam's 21st birthday. His best friends are here, joyously celebrating legal adulthood—except that none of them will ever quite be a legal adult. They were all born with serious birth defects. Each of their mothers took vitamins, ate right, had good prenatal care. We did everything in our power to have "perfect" babies. We found that our power didn't amount to much.

At the other end of the spectrum, my dog had surgery this week. The vet removed various tumors from his chubby old body, and he never really recovered. I spent the past few days sitting with his head on my lap, the only thing that seemed to make him comfortable. When a follow-up examination made it clear that Cookie had nothing in his future except suffering, I signed a form and put my arms around him as the vet added one more ingredient to his IV drip. Cookie set his sweet, soft head on my hand and died as he lived, with no fear and great love.

Birthdays and death days. Both remind us how little power we have. Both present us with infinite opportunities to either love or fear. To the extent that we choose love, the puniness of our material power is replaced by a power that comes not from us but through us. Judy and Linda accessed that power against the tide of social conditioning. Adam and his friends access it every day to live cheerfully with "disempowering" conditions. I felt it coursing through Cookie even as his body powered down, and I felt it in my own decision to let him go. Real power is usually unspectacular, a simple setting aside of fear that allows the free flow of love. But it changes everything.

Those who mistake violence for power are often surprised by this. Apartheid's architects didn't think twice about all the black women like Annie who were paid meager wages to "mind" white babies. They didn't realize that these women would do something revolutionary, choosing to see the infants of their oppressors not through the eyes of fear, as future enemies, but through the eyes of love, simply as babies. "For many white South Africans who were raised by black 'mothers,' there was no way on earth that apartheid could seem right to us," Judy told me. These women, and people like Judy, became heroes by insisting that love prevail in South Africa. Linda Hamilton became a hero by doing the same thing on an American sidewalk. And you can become a hero today, by choosing love over fear in any situation whatsoever.

Each of my clients eventually made the shift: In Mindy's case, empowerment took the form of staging an intervention for her daughter. Denise used her power to leave her hated job, even in today's scary economy. Paula checked into a hotel for three days of rest, then returned to her family with the determination that her own needs counted as much as anyone else's. Each of them felt the power of compassion flowing through them as they aligned themselves with love.

Power comes from actions like these, and the infinite small choices between love and fear. Today, pay close attention: Are you following the gripping energy of fear or the liberating energy of love? My own to-do list includes writing this column, calling clients, answering approximately 4,687,977 e-mails, and preparing a speech. Instead, I allowed myself to choose what my heart dictated. I baked a cake for five "handicapped" young people, and held on to a very old beagle while I let him go. It might not look like much from the outside, but I know power when I feel it.

AUGUST 2009

# When You *Should* Hold a Grudge

*Stood up by a friend? Let down by your sister?*
*Thrown for a loop by a coworker? The right-size grudge*
*can shield you from just about anything.*

I n 1988 Bette Midler's production company released the film *Beaches,* a moving homage to friendship and forgiveness. It may seem a bit odd, then, that the Divine Miss M.'s corporate motto was "We hold a grudge." Can love, forgiveness, and holding grudges really go together? Yes, they can—depending on how you define grudge.

Some people will hold a bitter grudge against anyone who looks at them cross-eyed. "Suzy made a 'dumb blonde' joke," a friend fumes. "Well, I'm blonde. As far as she knows. That's it, Suzy is dead to me!"

This is like donning full-on plate armor in response to a playful slap: With anger so heavy and disproportionate, you may end up collapsed on the battlefield wearing an outfit the size, weight, and consistency of a Toyota Yaris. If you're in a constant mouth-foaming rage at someone, get away and get a shrink. But if you simply find your mood dipping whenever you encounter a certain person, I suggest holding a grudge.

A good grudge is simply an acknowledgment of another person's foibles—it keeps you at a safe emotional distance from people who could mess up your life. Depending on the person, you might hold a grudge as light as a parasol or as solid as a titanium shield. Here, in order of severity, are descriptions of people who deserve to be held at bay:

## Planarian People

A planarian is a flatworm, one of the lowest life-forms that can be considered an animal. There are—search your mind or your cell phone contact list, and you'll see I'm right—human beings whose EQs stopped evolving at the planarian level. They aren't evil; they're just devoid of emotional intelligence. Once you've identified the planarian people in your life, choosing to bear a very light grudge toward them can spare you immense frustration. I was reminded of this by clients Jody and Ralph, who consulted me as a couple.

"Ralph's so insensitive," Jody complained. "Whenever I'm upset, he just says, 'Harsh, dude' and wanders away."

"What else can I do?" Ralph didn't sound insolent, just puzzled.

"You can talk to me about my feelings," said Jody.

Ralph looked at her as if she'd smacked him with a carp. "I don't understand," he mumbled.

Clearly, he didn't.

Ralph—and I say this lovingly—is a planarian. It isn't his fault, and it's not going to change. You can work a lifetime trying to make flatworms perceptive, intuitive, or wise, but the best they can do is, frankly, pathetic. Bearing this in mind is a form of grudge-holding that actually allows you to interact with them calmly. Instead of feeling towering rage at their emotional clumsiness, roll your eyes, mutter "planarian," and relax. Jody learned to do this with Ralph. They soon broke up but remained golf buddies. When Ralph fails to respond in a sensitive way to her emotions, Jody thinks "planarian," and takes her troubles elsewhere. This tiny semblance of a grudge will keep you from wasting your life in the hopes that people will be more evolved than they are.

## Three-Strikers

My favorite therapist taught me something I call the "three strike" rule: If you not only have a bad experience with a person but also hear worrisome reports about that person from three totally unrelated sources, you need to carry a protective grudge that says, "I don't quite trust you."

For example, I was once approached by a freelance TV producer I'll call Fred, who wanted to create a life-coaching reality show. During a meeting with a network executive, I was startled to hear Fred lie. Later he explained breezily, "You have to say what you have to say." This, as my daughters sometimes put it, did not gruntle me. But despite my disgruntlement, I dismissed the incident.

Within a week, by pure coincidence (or was it?), three people mentioned to me that they knew Fred. One was a woman he'd dated, another a colleague, a third his sister's high school buddy—and all of them delicately mentioned "honesty issues." Three strikes, plus one bad experience of my own, meant I put on a psychological Kevlar vest. I told Fred I'd decided not to work with him, and immediately felt much more relaxed.

## Gaslighters

I've learned through creepy experience that when I start inexplicably doubting myself around a specific person, it's time to hold a good constructive grudge. Me? I doubt myself constantly (rethinking impulse purchases, lying awake listening to myself wrinkle, and so on), but what I'm talking about is a much more unsettling self-doubt: the kind that surfaces when reality seems to bend and sway around a certain someone, when my recollections don't jibe with what that person claims and their stories glide smoothly around any factual inaccuracies I may point out.

Flurries of this dizzy sensation surround individuals who have secrets and hidden agendas. Psychologists use the term *gaslighting* to describe this type of systematic lying — an allusion to an old movie in which a man drives his wife to question her sanity by telling her odd lies and manipulating the level of gaslight in the house so that she keeps seeing lights dim for no reason.

When this happens to you, you've officially reached a "hard hat" area. If you don't bear a protective grudge against a gaslighter, you really might go nuts.

Consider Cindy. She worked alongside Danielle for months before noticing she felt strangely ungrounded at the office. "I doubted myself in ways I never had before," Cindy told me. "Eventually I realized that I always felt most confused after dealing with Danielle." Things got so bad that Cindy (feeling sheepish and paranoid) called one of Danielle's former employers to ask how he'd interacted with her. Surprise! Cindy discovered that the job on Danielle's résumé never existed. Kicking into sleuth mode, Cindy discovered that much of Danielle's résumé was fiction.

Now, this took place in a corporate environment, which explains what happened next: nothing. Cindy's supervisor, not wanting to admit she'd hired a deceitful loser, advised Cindy to ignore Danielle's flagrant fraud. "Don't hold a grudge," said the boss. Cindy disobeyed. Thenceforth, she worked with Danielle the way a bomb squad works with explosives, always questioning Danielle's fishy-sounding versions of the truth rather than her own sanity. When

Danielle (inevitably) did get fired, the manager who hadn't wanted to deal with the problem caught a lot of heat. Cindy, thanks to her light but resilient grudge, was scorch-free.

## Les Pitiables

Still wearing that hard hat? It's time to add work gloves and safety goggles, and perhaps jump in the reinforced driver's cage of a bulldozer. We're about to discuss the most danger- ous people of all: *les pitiables*. According to Martha Stout, PhD, an expert on sociopathy who taught at Harvard Medi- cal School for more than two decades, the key to recognizing sociopaths is that they consistently mess up other people's lives while actively soliciting pity. Most people don't want to be pitied, but sociopaths adore it. If you consistently feel pity for someone who causes you many problems, develop and bear a protective grudge. Now.

For example, Lucy's sister Sue was a walking disas- ter area. When she borrowed Lucy's car, it got rear-ended. When she babysat Lucy's children, the kids set fire to the curtains. When Lucy gave her sister money (Sue was always broke), the cash got lost or stolen. Through it all, Sue's mis- ery made Lucy's heart ache with pity.

Can you say "huge red flag"?

Sue was plying the sociopathic trade of getting Lucy to pity her for the very things she did to mess up Lucy's life. Finally, Lucy learned to hold a healthy grudge: She stopped buying into Sue's woeful stories, leaving children with her, or giving her money. She still loved Sue, but she wasn't willing to risk having her house go up in flames.

## The Hyde Transformers

A final reason for holding a grudge is what I call a visit from Mr. Hyde. Your instincts will tell you to react to such events by putting emotional distance between you and any person who displays the capacity to be truly monstrous—even if, most of the time, these people are jovial Dr. Jekylls.

Kelly's new boss, Cheryl, was funny, charismatic, and smart. True, she often showed up late for meetings, or seemed not to remember promises, but Kelly admired Cheryl in spite of those things. So she was shocked—actually, everyone was shocked—when Cheryl suddenly lost it during a staff meeting.

"We were discussing something insignificant," Kelly remembered. "I don't even recall what it was that set her off." But Kelly will never forget Cheryl's behavior. "She started screaming at us, saying we were all working together to 'bring her down.' Her face was bright red. She was sputtering. Then she turned on one woman who'd recently had a miscarriage, and said, 'You put that lump of tissue in your uterus ahead of me.' Our jaws were on the floor. That was just way beyond the pale."

On this bizarre note, Cheryl dismissed the meeting. A few hours later, she walked through the office chatting, so charming and relaxed that Kelly began to wonder if the tantrum really happened.

Kelly tried to rationalize Cheryl's behavior. "I thought maybe she had a brain tumor or something." But Kelly couldn't explain it away. Cheryl hadn't been just moody; she had been extraordinarily cruel. "Even in my worst mood," Kelly told me, "I would never have said something like that."

Wisely, Kelly held a grudge. She regarded Cheryl as she would a wild animal, one that could be calm and playful one moment, savage and destructive the next. There may be infinite explanations for such erratic behavior, but an explanation is not a reason to drop your armor. On most days, for example, Jeffrey Dahmer didn't kill or eat anyone. But the times he did made society hold a grudge against him. Forever. If someone in your life is genuinely monstrous part of the time—even once—be leery all the time. Wear your grudge armor. It could prevent catastrophe.

Having laid out the kinds of people who are best managed with caution, alertness, and the dexterity of a rattlesnake wrangler, I still think unconditional love and forgiveness are saintly qualities, ones we should all cultivate. If you need to be reminded of this, rent *Beaches* and watch it with your best friend. You'll cry your eyes out. Then dig in and talk about the human planarians in your life, the people who've struck out three times, the gaslighters, the pity mongers, and the Dr. Jekyll/Mr. Hyde transformers. Such talk keeps your grudges light and strong, the way God intended. Or at least how Miss M. intended. Which is divine enough for me.

# The
# Information Superflood

## Stay Afloat In A Sea of Texts, Tweets, and E-Mails

Is your life on track? Not so long ago, this question seemed eminently sensible. Everyone was trying to get on track, stay on track, move further down the track. We all chugged along like Thomas the Tank Engine, making scheduled station stops (schools, corporations, banks) to pick up the usual cargo (education, job, house) and passengers (friends, spouses, children). A divorce, illness, or job loss constituted catastrophic derailment. Everyone's goal was to claim, "You betcha, my life's on track!"

Today that answer makes no sense. Because, honey, there is no track. Not anymore. We're living through the most dramatic era of change in human history. A flood of new technologies and accompanying social transitions has altered everything. It's not just that we're on the receiving end of a torrent of messages, texts, and e-mails. The way we interact and build relationships has been turned upside down; whole careers and industries have been swept away. There's so much to do, to know, to learn, to master—and the floodwaters are rising.

To negotiate this new normal, we don't need locomotives. We need kayaks.

Now, it's not easy, letting go of the *chugga-chugga,* iron-engine mind-set. Kayaking, after all, is much less stable than riding a train, but these days, that's a huge advantage. This new approach allows you to go with the flow of change, turn quickly in any direction to avoid danger or pursue opportunity, pop upright again after you've gone under entirely (try doing that on a train).

Once you've learned a few paddling skills, you'll find that your nimble craft can ride the tide of change, accessing all sorts of interesting places and things no train could ever reach.

### Paddling Skill #1
## Don't Swallow the River

I've noticed that people who are still in train-track mode try to handle every demand or request that reaches them. That's like trying to drink the Nile. You just can't do everything. You shouldn't try. When your to-do list threatens to spill over, examine every item on it while asking two questions:

*1. Is this task absolutely necessary to keep my life afloat?*

*2. Does this task buoy me up emotionally?*

If the answer to either of these questions is yes, do the deed. If not, do nothing. Let that problem or opportunity float past you. Wave and smile, if you like, but don't bring inessential, unpleasant things on board. Your kayak isn't big enough. Anything unnecessary could sink you.

Right now my various mailboxes—voice, paper, and electronic—contain about 120 messages waiting to be answered. Today, about 15 of those messages—ten from work, five from loved ones—are essential to keep my professional and personal life from sinking. A couple more are from funny friends; they'll make me laugh. I'll get to those 17 messages today. The others, later. Maybe. I've found that important messages tend to bob along beside me, bonking against my kayak, until I get to them.

Each day, ask those two river-runner's questions about every request or assignment you encounter. Do the things that are absolutely necessary or make you happy. Let everything else drift away. If you overlook something important, you can always paddle over to it later, or snag something similar floating by. That's one of the joys of the crazy, fluid world we've created.

Paddling Skill #2
## Find Your Water Tribe

So that addresses the incoming flood, but what about the oceans of data beyond your in-box? Somewhere out there is the specific help, advice, and knowledge that's crucial to your life. The question is how to find it without getting carried out to sea.

Fortunately, modern communication technology greatly facilitates something called the wisdom of crowds. Simply put, when many diverse people answer a question (say, guessing the number of jelly beans in a jar), the mathematical average of all the responses is more likely to be accurate than any single response.

We're able to access this knowledge better than any other group of humans in history. When my son, Adam, was prenatally diagnosed with Down syndrome more than 20 years ago, no one around me knew what to say. I agonized, grieved, and feared without much social support.

This was before Google.

You see, the algorithm that makes Google work is also what makes it a good indicator of crowd wisdom. Just now, I Googled "prenatal diagnosis Down syndrome" for the very first time. The third article on the screen said, "Advice for women whose baby will be born with Down syndrome often comes from a perspective of misinformation and discouragement rather than celebration."

Celebration!

How different my life would've been if Google had existed on the day Adam was diagnosed. A wise, diverse, knowledgeable crowd would've been there—right there!—to counsel and support me better than my friends possibly could.

Today's information flood can be very kind. If you need to know which of the 12,000 recipes for healthful but tasty chicken are actually nutritious and delicious, consult the crowds. If you're looking for the best place to meet people who share your love of nude pot-throwing, start typing. Same goes for when you have to figure out what's happening in your industry, your neighborhood, your cable TV system. You'll gather not just the facts you need but the support and advice you never knew was out there.

## Paddling Skill #3
### Make Computers Your BFFs or FOFs

At this point, I should mention I have the computer skills of a hamster. So in 2006, I asked a computer scientist client to teach me to build a Web site. During the following months, my brain felt like a raisin on fire as I tried to fathom HTML, JavaScript, encryption software, and so on. It was like learning Swahili...in Turkish.

Maddeningly, my kids mastered this technology effortlessly. Children love Water World. Their brains are almost 100 percent "fluid intelligence," absorbing new skills fast. Adults rely on the "crystallized intelligence" stored in memory, which has been perfectly useful in the past—hey, why reinvent the wheel every day? Ha ha! Except now the wheels have come off. They're at the bottom of Davy Jones's locker. Here's the hard truth: Suck it up and deal. Learn to use computers.

I dish this out because I can take it. I spent nightmare months achieving minimal computer competency, losing all muscle tone except in my mouse-clicking finger, developing acne and insomnia. At one point I became so deeply geeky that I completely broke my eyeglasses, and the only way to use them was to packing-tape the lenses to my face. Which, God help me, I did.

It was so worth it.

If your head exploded at the idea of stapling yourself to a chair for months on end, you may never have a BFF in your computer. Okay, make computers your FOFs—friends of friends. Find computer lovers (your son, your sister, your minister) and exploit them ruthlessly. Get their help sending e-mail, setting up a blog, finding information, watching "stupid pet tricks playing dead." In fact, do that last one right now. Seriously. I'll wait.

See? It really is worth making friends with computers, or at the very least making friends with their friends. You'll find this is your basic paddling technique. Now you just have to learn how to steer your kayak.

Paddling Skill #4
## Site Your Purpose

One rainy night long ago, I was fleeing a PTA meeting in my minivan when I drove into a puddle that turned out to be four feet deep. The motor went eerily silent just as the vehicle became waterborne and began floating sideways. In the quiet, I heard a still, small voice within me. It said, "I hate PTA meetings, and I hate this %@&ing minivan."

In that moment, I was steering my life. By articulating what I hated, I began articulating what I loved—not the train-station life of a PTA mom but a kayaking life where I kept my kids home from school to watch YouTube. A life where adults would pay me to say, "Your true purpose is whatever makes you feel most joyful. Try steering toward that."

It's advice I've taken myself: During the months I was obsessed with computers, I felt very much "in the flow." The obsession vanished as inexplicably as it arrived, but it left me tech savvy enough to do research that informs my work—and manage a team that trains life coaches all over the world. Who knew the current would carry me there? I didn't. But I must say: Mama like.

I'm certainly not the only middle-aged mom to use current innovations for career development. Paula, a teacher, thought she'd never get to travel—until she did a deep dive online and discovered something called "location independent lifestyle." She's found jobs all over the world doing teacher-training workshops.

I've just come across another interesting story: Gina is—I kid you not—a massage therapist for dogs. I know this because (a) it says so on her Web site and (b) she's currently in my living room with our golden retriever, Bjorn, who's recovering from knee surgery. I can hear the strains of Enya from Gina's portable CD player, smell the aromatic ointments that have put Bjorn into a bliss-coma. A ridiculous luxury? I thought so, too, until I learned that a massaged dog heals faster. Gina saves money I'd otherwise spend on more vet appointments. I'm thrilled she paddled her kayak toward what gives her joy (though not as thrilled as Bjorn).

Right now, as best you can, write a statement of purpose for your life. If this feels impossible, there are Web sites created specifically to guide you through the process. I'm sure your minister will be glad to help you find them. If you need an example, my purpose statement today (I revise it often) is "To remain in continuous conscious awareness of the one Life in which all singular lives exist." Yesterday it was "To survive until bedtime." Your purpose statement can be grand or silly, as long as it rings true. It is to your kayak life what tracks were to trains: It determines your direction.

This column can't begin to describe the infinite opportunities you'll find as you navigate today's vast seas of possibility. If you learn basic paddling skills and steer by your inner purpose instead of predetermined social tracks, you'll have a joyful voyage. Maybe you'll meet your soul mate online, earn a degree at a distance, start a virtual business, or do something no one's even named yet.

These days, I'm not trying to read the future. I'm just paddling along my own trajectory as a coach, so I can pay BFFs to run my Web site (I'm now the site's FOF). I'm paddling by downloading instructions to help me call my daughter in Japan, on a cell phone that can play a thousand songs and show me satellite photos of almost anyplace on Earth.

Where will this white-water change take us next? My imagination doesn't stretch that far. I'm content to ride the tide. My own little kayak of a life can take me anywhere I need to go.

MARCH 2010

# How to Solve a Thorny Problem

*We're used to living in an either-or world—but when it comes to yes-or-no dilemmas, the most powerful thing you can ask is: What if both answers are true?*

"At first I thought Jack was just a rebound dater wanting to make a conquest," said Fiona over dinner with her girlfriends. "But he's called every day since our first date, and he's really sweet. He remembers my favorite song, he reads my blog—I think we really connected."

"Sounds like a dream come true," said Judith.

"On the other hand," Fiona countered, "he talks about his ex-girlfriend a lot, and he started hinting about sex five minutes after we met."

"Bad sign," Kathleen said. "Don't let the whole 'favorite song' thing fool you. He's just a player. He's thinking, 'Oh, yeah, I'm all that.'"

"What if both things are true?" This came from Deborah, who'd been listening silently in the corner. "Maybe he's a man-slut with a bruised ego trying to get someone in the sack, and he's a thoughtful person who really likes you."

The pregnant pause that followed could have given birth to triplets. When the conversation resumed, it was suddenly...deep. If the guy in question could be a combination of seemingly opposite traits, might not the same be true in other instances? Could Judith's recent job loss also be a stroke of great luck? Was Kathleen's workaholism both vaunting ambition and a humble desire to serve? And what about all those politicians and athletes—could they truly have the ideals of angels in their hearts and the morals of goats in their pants?

Uh...yes. Think of dilemmas like these as dual-emmas. Unlike standard-issue questions, dualistic dilemmas confuse people by leading to two apparently true but contradictory conclusions. Maybe you've found this in your own life: Perhaps your marriage is both wonderful and terrible, your job both wretched and stimulating, your worst habit both destructive and helpful. Reconciling these apparent brain-benders seems impossible, but if you understand the dynamics of dualism, you can transform bewildering dilemmas into sources of insight.

## On the Horns of a Dual-emma

There are two kinds of people in the world: those who divide everyone into two kinds of people, and those who don't. The tendency to dichotomize is stubbornly pervasive in human thought. Maybe this is because it presents decision-making in its simplest form. In evolutionary terms, this method has obvious advantages. Commit to one choice and you're done. If you're an early human on the savanna, you're better off fearing all snakes than having to closely examine each specimen for venom glands.

Even in our more nuanced world, this approach still works. You don't need the company of a snake to thrive, so you can avoid them all. But things become complicated when you get what a nurse friend of mine calls a mixed IV drip of essential fluids and poison—when a person or situation seems to provide necessary things like love and comfort but is also the source of pain and upset.

Confronted with such dualities, most of us try to choose between them. Friends and advisers weigh in on each option—and both camps make sense. Your instinct is to hunker down and figure out which is the "right" answer. After all, how else will you decide to stay or divorce, quit or stick with it? But limiting ourselves to one answer means we often stop seeing what's actually happening, and we make decisions based on labels instead: "The guy is a player, so no date," or "This friendship is dysfunctional—begone!" This strategy feels right...until the guy or the friend does something truly sweet, gives you the kindness and affection you love and need, and there you are, spiked again on the opposing horns of the dual-emma.

The problem is that an *either-or* thought process won't resolve a *both-and* reality. This point was once driven home for me by a client I'll call Janet, who brought her teenage daughter "Angela" to a coaching session. Angela tearfully confessed, "I've been doing drugs and having sex with boys." Janet calmly replied, "No, you haven't; you're a good girl."

Then she turned to me and asked, "What's the real issue here?" The real issue was that Janet had no way to deal with the possibility that Angela was a good girl who also did drugs and had sex. In Janet's mind, a good person, like her honor-roll daughter, has no bad characteristics. Unable to bridge the divide, Janet went mind-blind to Angela.

Like Janet, we make judgments about all kinds of people, deciding, for instance, that surely the legendary athlete with his boyish smile and beautiful family would never succumb to roid rage. Or that the mousy homemaker next door would never have a torrid e-mail affair. We're not only shocked when those assumptions don't hold up, we're unsure how to handle the new information.

The only option for Janet, for you, for anyone who's confronted with two apparently opposite sets of data, is to blast apart the mental dichotomies that organize our minds and drive our behavior. How do you respond to the harassing boss who gives you wonderful, career-building feedback but throws degrading tantrums? Or the friend whose loyalty never fails, except that she flakes and forgets to pick you up after your appendectomy? Are they good people you want in your life or jerks you should avoid?

Yes.

If you scrutinize your own life, you'll find you do plenty of things that violate the dichotomies in your mind. I certainly do. We're considerate, selfless, and clever (except for the times we aren't). Or we're luckless losers (not counting the infinite things that go right for us every day). This is the problem with either-or thinking: It keeps us removed from reality, and it requires that we spend a lot of time and energy convincing ourselves that life is one particular way (and burying evidence that doesn't jibe with that view). More important, it will never feel truthful or satisfying—because it leads to an answer that's only half-right.

## What to Do When Both Things Are True

In mathematics, one kind of problem that sends the mind bouncing back and forth between seemingly opposite truths is called a strange loop. The only possible way out is for mathematicians to use a metastatement that draws attention to the loop itself. In the case of a dualistic dilemma, the metastatement is "Oh, I'm using either-or thinking when both-and thinking is required."

What makes a both-and mindset so powerful is that it takes you beyond the two choices you thought you had. It opens up new, previously unseen possibilities and opportunities.

There is one caveat to all dual-emma relationships: If you or the other person involved can't or won't admit the whole truth—"Yup, I have a Dr. Jekyll side, but there's also a Mr. Hyde in here"—the relationship will become increasingly dysfunctional.

If both parties can discuss the full range of their behavior, however, almost any relationship can work. You just need to follow three basic steps:

### 1. Set Boundaries That Correspond to The Worst of Times

According to Abraham Maslow's famous hierarchy of needs, the very first psychological need we have is to know we're safe. That's why, when you're around someone who's both good and bad, your first step is one that may seem a bit cruel: When times are good, establish limits that prepare you to deal with the relationship when times are bad. This is how you'll keep from being blindsided by something that—hello—you've already learned.

If your boss is a sweetheart who has tantrums, agree with him during a reasonable moment that you'll both observe certain rules of engagement: "No shouting, or we go to our offices and cool down until everyone's feeling civil." If your supportive friend tends to space out, ask someone more dependable to do a crucial favor. If your loving mom has bouts of negligence, don't entrust her with your twin toddlers.

## 2. Focus Your Appreciation on the Best of Times

In his book *What Happy People Know,* psychologist Dan Baker, PhD, describes an elderly woman named Marlene reminiscing about her beloved late husband. When Baker said he must have been a good man, Marlene said, "He was a womanizer and a drunk. A real pain in the butt." She simply chose to focus on the deep and abundant love they'd shared. Baker considered this choice a key to her health and happiness.

Notice there was no denial in Marlene's image of her husband; she acknowledged all his faults and refused to gauze over his memory. And then she chose to bask in his best legacy rather than his terrible betrayals. Setting strong boundaries frees us to take this attitude—and it allows us to access the happiness that's available right now.

## 3. Remain Calm While You Explore Your Options

That phrase—"right now"—is important. When you're dealing with a dual-emma, focus on being fully present with what's happening in this moment, rather than assuming past bad (or good) behavior predicts future consistency. This means alternating freely between the two previous steps. You don't want to spend your life anticipating your boss's next meltdown; neither do you want to assume that his jovial, charming behavior will last through the week. As you explore the scope of the other person's actions, you'll learn whether you can accept this particular mixed IV drip.

In Fiona's case, this meant realizing that, yes, Jack may be a player—and a really compatible match. Maybe, as Kathleen said, "he thinks he's all that" at some times but is grounded, affectionate, and responsive enough at others to make his occasional narcissism worth tolerating (with appropriate boundaries—"I'm going to watch TV while you preen, Jack dear. Call me when you're finished!").

As they contemplated Deborah's idea that a scoundrel could also be sincere, Fiona and her friends began, in the words of one yogi, "existing in continuous creative response to whatever was present"—in their love lives, their careers, their definition of self.

Try seeing your world and yourself this way, eyes open to whatever is before you, mind free of dichotomies. Are you good or bad, fragile or tough, wise or foolish? Yes. And so am I. What Jack thought about himself (at least according to Kathleen) is true of every human being. Oh, yeah. We're all that.

JULY 2010

# The 4-Step Plan to Get Your Life on Track

*If you're trying to figure out what to do with your one and only life, you need to stop thinking rationally— and go a little wild. Here is a powerful technique for discovering your next move.*

a t first I trusted my car's global positioning system— why not?—but soon its smooth voice began sounding like the homicidal computer HAL in *2001: A Space Odyssey*. "Turn left now," the GPS would command as I drove along a freeway, with concrete barriers to my left. "You have reached your destination," it would assure me after leading me to a warehouse full of prostitutes and crack dealers. Once my kids programmed it to speak French, the GPS abandoned all pretense of helpfulness and began directing me southward in any and all circumstances. Presumably it was heading for Mexico to escape fraud charges.

These days, listening to my clients talk about their careers reminds me how bewildered I was by my demon guidance machine. People wander aimlessly because the well-worn paths of yesteryear—and by that I mean 2009—are disappearing, while strange new career options pop up before our frazzled brains can map them. The more new technologies and job descriptions have entered everyday life, the more my clients tend to become confused and over-whelmed, finding themselves facing a dead end. Like most of us who have no clue about how to get to where we want, they long for a voice of authority, a career GPS, that will spell out the exact route to a thrilling and fulfilling position. Although they keep beavering away at a solution, research-ing their options and seeking the advice of people with hot new ideas for them ("Use this career-finder app!" "What you need is a website!" "Blog, blog, blog!"), people end up in my office more muddled than ever. They tell me things like:

> *"There's so much going on, and it sounds exciting to me, but I feel paralyzed about which new thing to follow up on."*

> *"I keep reading about all these new opportunities, but I don't really understand them, and I'm afraid I'm being left behind."*

*"I'd be happy to follow my passion . . . if only I knew what it was."*

*"I worry that if I commit to one career, I'll lose out on something better."*

If any of these sound like you, don't bother with classic career guides; like my GPS, they'll have you meandering in circles, stumped at dead ends, or just profoundly lost. The fact is, as we've become accustomed to our overmanaged, overstimulated 21st-century lives, we haven't realized that there might be another—decidedly low-tech—way to get onto the right path.

I suspect you've been advised to think rationally about your career decisions. That would be a big mistake. You might expect people with damage to the emotional parts of the brain, presumably free from the distractions of emotions, to be brilliant decision makers. Quite the opposite. Though they retain full use of their rational faculties, such patients are tragically indecisive, endlessly debating logical pros and cons, unable to choose any path. Their brains send out random, contradictory, and confusing directions, like my rogue GPS. It turns out that, as Jonathan Haidt writes in *The Happiness Hypothesis,* "it is only because our emotional brains work so well that our reasoning can work at all."

Although humans are the only beings on Earth with advanced linguistic skills, any animal with a brain has the automatic capacity to form preferences. It's an irrational sense of "Yes, this!" that takes a migrating goose a thousand miles to its perfect nesting ground, or a whale to its calving waters an ocean away. To find—or rather, design—your perfect career, you have to let your animal self lead you through a wilderness of choices. The way to do that is to make your rational mind not the master but the tracker of your own irrational instincts.

## Tracking Your Inner Animal

I was trudging down the traditional career path of academia when my students, weirdly, began offering to pay me for advice. I didn't think of it as a career path; I'd never heard the phrase "life coach," and if I had, I'd have gagged like a sommelier drinking Kool-Aid. But I loved my students, and I loved helping them build happy lives. My emotional self trotted cheerfully forward, enjoying the scenery, while my rational, verbal GPS argued, puzzled, and worried:

> Animal brain: *Me like this!*
> Rational brain: *But what are you doing?*
> Animal brain: *Me like this!*
> Rational brain: *Is it secure? Is it respectable?*
> Animal brain: *Me like this!*
> Rational brain: *Get a job, dammit!*

This process continues even now, with my animal self migrating through unknown territory as my logical mind struggles to make sense of where in God's name I'm going. How grateful I am to be familiar with what one expert describes to me as deductive/predictive animal tracking. It's helped me calm my nerves and follow my animal into a thousand joyful and productive career events I never dreamed possible.

Deductive/predictive tracking goes like this: Locate a clear footprint left by an animal you're trailing—a so-called hot track. Make an educated guess, based on the animal's previous behavior, about where the animal would probably have gone next. Proceed to that spot. Look for more tracks. If you find no tracks—if the trail runs cold—return to the last hot track, make another educated guess, and repeat. Using these steps, you can follow your wild self as it instinctively migrates toward your perfect career:

### Step 1. Discover your hot tracks.

Grab a pen and make a list of every time you remember being utterly, happily absorbed in an activity, no matter how odd. This focused attention is the hot track you're looking for, evidence that your animal self was here.

For example, my client Adeline loved helping her mother bake, playing doubles tennis, assisting her husband as he built his business, and raising money for AIDS research. Dora was happiest while shopping, throwing ceramic pots, and gardening. Lily loved singing in her church choir, going to parties, volunteering for political candidates, and working at a large marketing firm. Write your own list of hot tracks from the past.

*Step 2. Predict the next track.*

If you were tracking bison in the wild, you might notice they migrate along predictable grassy routes. Geese, by contrast, follow a route from one marshy area to another. To predict the next likely step for your inner animal, scan your environment for conditions that seem likely to foster that happy state of absorption, but are just outside your regular routine. Try an activity within that sphere to see if it's a hot track.

**WARNING:** Many people assume that a hot track is leading them toward a job directly related to that track. Unwittingly, they start heading to the nearest "logical career." For example, Adeline's love of baking initially led her to train as a pastry chef. Dora's shopping passion convinced her she should work as a retail buyer. Lily decided to run for office. Perfectly reasonable predictions—but all these trails froze. Adeline found culinary school boring, Dora loathed working with retailers, and Lily became exhausted and disillusioned running for city council. The lesson: Even if you're pursuing a course that's perfectly rational—a job that makes total sense on paper—emotions like boredom, hopelessness, anger, or anxiety mean the trail's gone cold.

*Step 3. Return to the last hot track and repeat step 2.*

Many of my clients continue endlessly on cold trails. Some cling to established career paths, imagining that the next promotion will bring happiness, despite the obvious lack of clear hot tracks such as enjoyment, fascination, or any heartfelt desire (apart from the wish to bang one's head against a wall). Others gallop along any path, without pausing to check whether it's one their animal prefers. Still other clients give up hope and plod along in so-so jobs. I can't say it enough: If your trail runs cold, return to your last hot track and test a new prediction.

When Adeline went back to her hot tracks and focused on the elements that connected them, she noticed her animal had left a trail of relationships. She loved working with strong, decisive partners. Dora's hot tracks always related to arranging colorful objects. Lily's hot tracks led to large, active groups; teamwork, not politics, was her bliss.

### Step 4. Follow your tracks wherever they lead.

You have to commit to following your animal—even if it seems to have the directional ability of my poltergeisted GPS. Trust me, your animal will eventually bring you to the job you were meant to do. Once Adeline realized her strong-partner theme, she teamed up with a friend running online boutiques for custom-designed clothing. Dora discovered that computer graphics let her assemble gorgeous color combinations with a few clicks. She's now a website designer. Lily agreed to organize a conference for an ex-coworker's business and enjoyed it so much, she began freelancing as an event planner.

Note that all these careers use new technologies, but technology was not the track. Adeline went looking for a business partner and just happened to find one with a "virtual" shop. Dora was surfing websites when she noticed that the colors of the sites themselves attracted her. Lily hated computers but loved using social networking to connect with people. All began with "What do I enjoy?" and proceeded to beat the bushes for their best-loved activities. New technologies simply facilitated their passions, which, as I used to tell my GPS, is what technology is meant to do.

As you track your career, remember that your inner animal is following primal instincts, not established paths that will necessarily impress your parents, spouse, and friends. Their expectations—and yours—are an outdated guidance system that will only send you sideways and, in my experience, due south. We live in an increasingly civilized, rational-minded, tech-obsessed world. It's time to break out: Let your wild self explore wild career ideas. Of course, if this makes you nervous, you can always go grovel for a low-paying version of that civilized job you loathed. But as the poet Mary Oliver puts it, "meanwhile...the world offers itself to your imagination, calls to you like the wild geese, harsh and exciting—over and over announcing your place in the family of things." Answer that call, following your instinct through the wilderness of career options, and your inner tracking system will take you to exactly the terrain that's right for you. Me like that!

NOVEMBER 2010

# 20 Questions That Could Change Your Life

*Finding the answers starts with posing the right questions—here are 20 to get you started.*

• 

f you're like most people, you became obsessed with questions around the age of 2 or 3, and scientists now know that continuing to ask them can help keep your mind nimble however old you eventually become. So when someone suggested I put together a list of the 20 most important questions we should all be asking ourselves, I was thrilled. Initially. Then I became confused about which questions to ask, because of course, as I soon realized, context is everything. In terms of saving your life, the key question is, "Did I remember to fasten my seat belt?" In terms of saving money, "How much do I need to retire before I'm 90?" is a strong contender. If daily usefulness is the point, "What'll I wear?" and "What should I eat first?" might lead the list. And for the philosophically minded, "To be or not to be?" really is the question.

Because I'm far too psychologically fragile to make sense of this subjective morass, I made the bold decision to pass the buck. The 20 questions that follow are based on "crowdsourcing," meaning I asked a whole mess of actual, free-range women what they thought every woman should ask herself. Thanks to all of you who sent in entries via social media. The questions included here are composites of those that were suggested most often, though I've mushed them together and rephrased some for brevity. Asking them today could redirect your life. Answering them every day will transform it.

### 1. What questions should I be asking myself?

At first I thought asking yourself what you should be asking yourself was redundant. It isn't. Without this question, you wouldn't ask any others, so it gets top billing. It creates an alert, thoughtful mind state, ideal for ferreting out the information you most need in every situation. Ask it frequently.

### 2. Is this what I want to be doing?

This very moment is, always, the only moment in which you can make changes. Knowing which changes are best for you comes, always, from assessing what you feel. Ask yourself many times every day if you like what you're doing. If the answer is no, start noticing what you'd prefer. Thus begins the revolution.

### 3. Why worry?

These two words, considered sincerely, can radically reconfigure the landscape of your mind. Worry rarely leads to positive action; it's just painful, useless fear about hypothetical events, which scuttles happiness rather than ensuring it. Some psychologists say that by focusing on gratitude, we can shut down the part of the brain that worries. It actually works!

### 4. Why do I like {cupcakes} more than I like {people}?

Feel free to switch out the words in brackets: You may like TV more than exercise, or bad boys more than nice guys, or burglary more than reading. Whatever the particulars, every woman has something she likes more than the somethings she's supposed to like. But forcing "virtues"—trying to like people more than cupcakes—drives us to vices that offer false freedom from oppression. Stop trying to like the things you don't like, and many vices will disappear on their own.

### 5. How do I want the world to be different because I lived in it?

Your existence is already a factor in world history—now, what sort of factor do you want it to be? Maybe you know you're here to create worldwide prosperity, a beautiful family, or one really excellent bagel. If your impressions are more vague, keep asking this question. Eventually you'll glimpse clearer outlines of your destiny. Live by design, not by accident.

## 6. How do I want to be different because I lived in this world?

In small ways or large, your life will change the world—and in small ways or large, the world will change you. What experiences do you want to have during your brief sojourn here? Make a list. Make a vision board. Make a promise. This won't control your future, but it will shape it.

## 7. Are {vegans} better people?

Again, it doesn't have to be vegans; the brackets are for you to fill in. Substitute the virtue squad that makes you feel worst about yourself, the one you'll never have the discipline to join, whether it's ultra-marathoners or mothers who never raise their voices. Whatever group you're asking about, the answer to this question is no.

## 8. What is my body telling me?

As I often say, my mind is a two-bit whore—by which I mean that my self-justifying brain, like any self-justifying brain, will happily absorb beliefs based on biases, ego gratification, magical thinking, or just plain error. The body knows better. It's a wise, capable creature. It recoils from what's bad for us, and leans into what's good. Let it.

### 9. How much junk could a chic chick chuck if a chic chick could chuck junk?

I believe this question was originally posed by Lao Tzu, who also wrote, "To become learned, each day add something. To become enlightened, each day drop something." Face it: You'd be better off without some of your relationships, many of your possessions, and most of your thoughts. Chuck your chic-chick junk, chic chick. Enlightenment awaits.

### 10. What's so funny?

Adults tend to put this question to children in a homicidal-sounding snarl, which is probably why as you grew up, your laughter rate dropped from 400 times a day (for toddlers) to the grown-up daily average of 15. Regain your youth by laughing at every possible situation. Then, please, tell us what's funny—about everyday life, about human nature, even about pain and fear. We'll pay you anything.

### 11. Where am I wrong?

This might well be the most powerful question on our list—as Socrates believed, we gain our first measure of intelligence when we first admit our own ignorance. Your ego wants you to avoid noticing where you may have bad information or unworkable ideas. But you'll gain far more capability and respect by asking where you're wrong than by insisting you're right.

## 12. What potential memories am I bartering, and is the profit worth the price?

I once read a story about a world where people sold memories the way we can sell plasma. The protagonist was an addict who'd pawned many memories for drugs but had sworn never to sell his memory of falling in love. His addiction won. Afterward he was unaware of his loss, lacking the memory he'd sold. But for the reader, the trade-off was ghastly to contemplate. Every time you choose social acceptance over your heart's desires, or financial gain over ethics, or your comfort zone over the adventure you were born to experience, you're making a similar deal. Don't.

## 13. Am I the only one struggling not to {fart} during {yoga}?

I felt profoundly liberated when this issue was raised on *Saturday Night Live*'s "Weekend Update." Not everyone does yoga, but *SNL* reminded me that everyone dreads committing some sort of gaffe. Substitute your greatest shame-fear: crying at work, belching in church, throwing up on the prime minister of Japan. Then know you aren't alone. Everyone worries about such faux pas, and many have committed them (well, maybe not the throwing up on PMs). Accepting this is a bold step toward mental health and a just society.

## 14. What do I love to practice?

Some psychologists believe that no one is born with any particular talent and that all skill is gained through practice. Studies have shown that masters are simply people who've practiced a skill intensely for 10,000 hours or more. That requires loving—not liking, *loving*—what you do. If you really want to excel, go where you're passionate enough to practice.

## 15. Where could I work less and achieve more?

To maximize time spent practicing your passions, minimize everything else. These days you can find machines or human helpers to assist with almost anything. Author Timothy Ferriss "batches" job tasks into his famous "four-hour workweek." My client Cindy has an e-mail ghostwriter. Another client, Angela, hired an assistant in the Philippines who flawlessly tracks her schedule and her investments. Get creative with available resources to find more time in your life and life in your time.

## 16. How can I keep myself absolutely safe?

Ask this question just to remind yourself of the answer: You can't. Life is inherently uncertain. The way to cope with that reality is not to control and avoid your way into a rigid little demi-life, but to develop courage. Doing what you long to do, despite fear, will accomplish this.

### 17. Where should I break the rules?

If everyone kept all the rules, we'd still be practicing cherished traditions like child marriage, slavery, and public hangings. The way humans become humane is by assessing from the heart, rather than the rule book, where the justice of a situation lies. Sometimes you have to break the rules around you to keep the rules within you.

### 18. So say I lived in that fabulous house in Tuscany, with untold wealth, a gorgeous, adoring mate, and a full staff of servants . . . then what?

We can get so obsessed with acquiring fabulous lives that we forget to live. When my clients ask themselves this question, they almost always discover that their "perfect life" pastimes are already available. Sharing joy with loved ones, spending time in nature, finding inner peace, writing your novel, plotting revenge—you can do all these things right now. Begin!

### 19. Are my thoughts hurting or healing?

Your situation may endanger your life and limbs, but only your thoughts can endanger your happiness. Telling yourself a miserable mental story about your circumstances creates suffering. Telling yourself a more positive and grateful story, studies show, increases happiness. Wherever you are, whatever you're doing, choose thoughts that knit your heart together, rather than tear it apart.

## 20. Really truly: Is this what I want to be doing?

It's been several seconds since you asked this. Ask it again. Not to make yourself petulant or frustrated—just to see if it's possible to choose anything, and I mean any little thing, that would make your present experience more delightful. Thus continues the revolution.

FEBRUARY 2011

# How to Tune In to the Voice Within

*Here's how to ignore the racket and understand how you really feel.*

This very day, two individuals are vying to be your personal adviser. The first, whose name is Fang, dresses in immaculate business attire, carries a briefcase full of neatly organized folders, and answers all e-mails instantly, via BlackBerry. In a loud, clear, authoritative voice, Fang delivers strong opinions about how you should manage your time. Fang's résumé is impressive: fantastic education, experience to burn.

The other candidate, Buddy, wears shorts, a tank top, and a rose tattoo. If you question the professionalism of this attire, Buddy just smiles. When you ask advice on a pressing matter, Buddy hugs you. There are almost no words on

Buddy's résumé (the few that do appear are jokes and song lyrics), and in the margins, Buddy has doodled pictures of chipmunks.

Who will you hire to advise you?

Yeah, that's what I used to think, too.

Long, long ago, as a teenager, I gave the name Fang to my socially conscious, verbal, educated mind. Buddy was what I called a perverse, disobedient aspect of my being, who apparently never evolved logical semantics and simply does not understand How Things Are Done Around Here. Fang is wary and suspicious, while Buddy ignores all caution in the pursuit of appealing experiences, like a puppy on LSD. In high school, I vowed to let only Fang run my life. A couple of decades later, I noticed something surprising: Though I generally did listen to Fang, it was Buddy who was always right.

When clients tell me they need to find their "inner voice," I suspect they're already listening to one: a loud, logical, convincing Fang-voice that echoes parents, teachers, priests, and angry personal trainers. You have no problem hearing this voice; the problem is, its counsel rarely leads to fulfillment. Yet you sense there's someone else knocking around in your psyche: someone whose counsel might make you happy—the kind of wise, primordial self I named Buddy. Unfortunately, Buddy is almost nonverbal, initially unimposing, and, from Fang's point of view, way too weird to trust. I believe one of the primary tasks of your life is to trust Buddy anyway. That means first learning to recognize true inner wisdom, and then opening yourself to its peculiar counsel.

## Noticing What Your Inner Wisdom Is and Is Not

Real wisdom is so different from what's drilled into us by most authority figures that we tend to go functionally blind to it. But even if you can't recognize your own wisdom, you can notice what it isn't. Compare this list of Buddy traits with their Fang opposites.

### Wisdom Is Sensory, Not Verbal

"It's not as though I hear a voice," says a friend of mine who's famous for her wisdom. "It's more like a little kid tapping me on the shoulder. It's something I feel."

In other words, while the voice of social conditioning manifests itself as a stream of thoughts in the head, wisdom often appears as emotions or physical sensations in the body. Brain-damaged patients who lose function in parts of the brain that register emotion may still understand the logic of a problem, but can no longer reason effectively or make advantageous decisions for themselves. The emotional centers of the brain, along with the elaborate bundle of nerves in your belly (the so-called gut brain), have been evolving far longer than language. And that system, more than logic, is exquisitely attuned to helping you navigate your way through life.

So if you're wondering whether a choice is wise or not, don't search your mind for a rational argument. Instead, hold each option in your attention, then feel its effect on your body and emotions. When something's wrong for you, you'll feel constriction and tightness. The wise choice leads to feelings of liberation, even exhilaration.

### Wisdom Is Calm, Not Fearful

The inner voice of social conditioning—that would be Fang—doesn't just speak in words; it shouts them. *"Do it my way!"* Fang shrieks. *"Do not screw this up!"* By contrast, inner wisdom is stillness itself. If you're waiting for wisdom to outscream paranoia, get comfortable. It's gonna be a long wait.

Instead, you might want to regard the thought stream in your brain as an annoying TV talk show playing in an upstairs apartment. Send your attention downstairs, to a place in the center of your chest where Buddy is smiling in the stillness. It helps to take some deep breaths. You may have to lie down. But as you feel for that stillness, the yawping from your brain will seem less important. As you begin to relax, you'll find yourself guided to do unexpected things. These may include just resting, often the single wisest choice.

### Wisdom Is Chosen, Not Forced

From infancy we're trained by adults who can force us to cooperate. Sometimes, indeed, we're trained so well that we begin to expect all instructions to come through coercion. *"You're crazy to want that!"* Fang shouts as you try to grow or enjoy life. "You don't deserve it!" "You'll fail!"

Meanwhile, your inner Buddy knocks gently, then waits to be invited in. Wisdom is far, far stronger than fear, but while fear gladly forces itself upon you, wisdom will do nothing of the kind. We can't be victims of wisdom: It must be chosen.

Stop and examine any frightening, ugly, or painful thought that customarily drives you. Ask yourself: *Really?* Is this really the kind of energy you want blaring through your inner space? If not, calmly state a truer thought: "You're wrong, Fang. I do deserve this, and even if I do fail, the world won't end."

Fang will not appreciate this. There will be shouting. But you'll gain wisdom every time you choose to believe the peaceful thoughts again—and again, and again, and again. Ultimately, this practice will enable you to take Fang less seriously. Then you can go out to play with Buddy, who's much more interesting.

## Following Your Inner Buddy

*Exercise 1: WWBD?*
Think of a challenging circumstance or difficult decision you happen to be facing right now—something that's been keeping you up at night. With this situation in mind, write

the first answer that comes up when you ask yourself the following questions. Don't overthink the answers. In fact, don't think about the answers at all—just blurt.

## With regard to your difficult situation...

*What would calm do now?*

*What would peace do now?*

*What would relaxation do now?*

(Note: I don't include "What would love do now?" because so many people have such misguided interpretations of love. They think love would sacrifice its own happiness, or throw a tantrum, or hide in an ex-boyfriend's garage wearing nothing but night-vision goggles and a leopard-print thong.)

The more often you ask yourself these strange questions, the more open you become to the gentle energy of your own inner wisdom. When you feel your body begin to let go of tension, you know you're headed in a wise direction.

And *that's* what Buddy would do.

*Exercise 2: Nightmare Board, Wisdom Board*
Perhaps you've heard of vision boards: collages you assemble from pictures of things that appeal to you. Most of us go through life carrying something similar in our minds—

except that instead of pictures that appeal to us, they're crowded with pictures that torment and terrify us. I call these nightmare boards.

Your nightmare board, curated, assembled, and prominently displayed by your inner Fang, contains images of everything that frightens and upsets you, including all your most hideously painful experiences. Fang is continuously adding new pictures to the board and lovingly retouching the old ones.

Here's a radical assignment: Make your nightmare board real. Glue up some actual images of every frightening thought that haunts you. But don't stop there. When you're finished, you're going to make another board. This new board must contain three or more images that contradict every picture on the nightmare board. For example, if your nightmare board shows a devastating oil spill, your vision board might feature three photographs of people tenderly swabbing oil-coated ducks. For every image of violence, come up with three examples of loving kindness; for every crisis, find three beautiful, ordinary moments of calm.

When you're finished, ceremoniously shred, burn, or otherwise trash Fang's nightmare board. Then put your wisdom board where you can see it. Focusing on hope in a world of fear isn't naive. It's the irrational essence of wisdom.

### Exercise 3: Vocab Rehab
Take ten minutes and write a description of your life—stream of consciousness, no self-judgment, no editing. Then

go over your description, looking for every word that carries frightening or painful associations. These words have more power than you might think. Studies show that after focusing on words having to do with aging, people walk more slowly; when they see words associated with anger, they're more likely to be rude.

This phenomenon is called affective priming, but it works both ways. You can use it to connect with your inner wisdom by changing every stressful word in your self-description to something more freeing, relaxing, or exhilarating. If you wrote "I'm nervous," see whether "I'm excited" may also fit. The word unsure could be replaced by open. As you change your story, Fang's voice will begin to soften, and the peace that comes from your wiser inner voice will begin to arise.

## Practice Makes Permanent

All these exercises can divert your attention from bossy, self-righteous Fang and help you appreciate the brilliance of your inner Buddy. Wisdom will never be the loud, obvious one in this odd couple. It will never shout down its opposition or barge in uninvited. But each time you choose wisdom as your adviser, you come closer to making the choice a way of life. Trust me, that's advice you want to take.

# How to Love More
# by Caring Less

*How do you get your nearest and dearest to change their behavior? Simple: Stop giving a damn what they do.*

"Now my whole family is abusing me!" said Loretta, a client at a women's resource center where I volunteered back in the '90s. "If I leave my husband, it'll just be out of the frying pan and into the fire."

"Are you—" I cut myself off before finishing my thought, which was, "Are you crazy?" Just the week before, I'd participated in an intervention where Loretta's family had urged her to leave her battering husband, Rex. Each person had expressed enormous love for and protectiveness toward Loretta. Now she thought they were all abusers? Huh?

"They're just like Rex," she said. "You saw it. They judge me. They criticize me. Nothing I do is enough for them."

I opened my mouth, then closed it. Opened then closed it again. I kept that up for about a minute, like a perplexed goldfish, as I groped for the right thing to say. It killed me that Loretta was interpreting her family's desire to rescue her as criticism and judgment. But even as I tried to come up with the kindest possible phrasing for "What the hell is wrong with you?" I knew my question would come across like a slap.

That's when it dawned on me that Loretta had a point. No, her family wasn't abusing her the way Rex did—and yet in its own way, their treatment of her must have felt like an attack. They weren't accepting her as she was. They needed her to change. They raised their voices, made demands, pushed hard. And their intense negative emotions were triggering her fear and defensiveness.

It was in the midst of processing all this that I suddenly heard myself say, "Well, Loretta, I just love you. I don't care what happens to you."

The statement shocked me as it left my lips. But even as I mentally smacked myself upside the head, a funny thing happened: Loretta visibly relaxed. I could feel my own anxiety vanishing, too, leaving a quiet space in which I could treat Loretta kindly. It was true—I really didn't care what happened to her. No matter what she did, I wouldn't love her one bit less.

Since then I've found that loving without caring is a useful approach—I'd venture to say the best approach—in most relationships, especially families. If you think that's coldhearted, think again. It may be time you let yourself love more by caring less.

## Detached Attachment

To care for someone can mean to adore them, feed them, tend their wounds. But *care* can also signify sorrow, as in "bowed down by cares." Or anxiety, as in "Careful!" Or investment in an outcome, as in "Who cares?" The word *love* has no such range of meaning: It's pure acceptance. Watching families like Loretta's taught me that caring—with its shades of sadness, fear, and insistence on specific outcomes—is not love. In fact, when care appears, unconditional love often vanishes.

When my son was first diagnosed with Down syndrome, I cared so much that my fear for his future overshadowed my joy at his existence. Now that I couldn't care less how many chromosomes the kid has, I can love him boundlessly. For you, loving without caring might mean staying calm when your sister gets divorced, or your dad starts smoking again, or your husband is laid off. You may think that in such situations not getting upset would be unloving. But consider: If you were physically injured, bleeding out, would you rather be with someone who screamed and swooned, or someone who stayed calm enough to improvise a tourniquet? Real healing, real love comes from people who are both totally committed to helping—and able to emotionally detach.

This is because, on an emotional level, our brains are designed to mirror one another. As a result, when we're anxious and controlling, other people don't respond with compliance; they reflect us by becoming—press the button when you get the right answer—anxious and controlling. Anger elicits anger, fear elicits fear, no matter how well meaning we may be. When Loretta's family insisted she leave Rex, she insisted on staying. When I told her I loved her without caring what happened, she mirrored my relaxation. That's when she began to request and absorb the advice I was now welcome to give.

## Free to Be . . . Carefree

If you want to try loving without caring—and by now I hope you do—here's how to get there. Just be sure to buckle up. This may be a bumpy ride.

### 1. Choose a Subject
Think of a person you love, but about whom you feel some level of anxiety, anger, or sadness.

### 2. Identify What This Person Must Change
   to Make You Happy
Think about how your loved one must alter herself or her behavior before you can be content. Complete the sentence

below by filling in the name of your loved one, the thing(s) you want this person to change, and the way you'd feel if the change occurred:

If _____ would only _____, then I could feel _____.

### 3. Accept a Radical Reality

Now scratch out the first clause of the sentence you just wrote, so all that remains is:

I could feel _____.

That last sentence, oh best beloved, is the truth. It is the whole truth. Yes, your loved one's cooperation would be lovely, but you don't absolutely need it to experience any given emotional state. This is incredibly hard to accept—it would be so easy to feel good if others would just do what we want, right? Nevertheless, you can feel sane even if your crazy-making brother stays crazy. You can feel peaceful even if your daughter robs a bank. If Helen Keller could write, after growing up deaf and blind, "I seldom think about my limitations, and they never make me sad," then you can find a way to be happy even if your mother never does stop correcting your grammar.

Accepting that this is possible—that you can achieve a given emotional state even if a loved one doesn't conform to your wishes—is the key step to loving without caring. I'm not saying that such acceptance will make you instantly content. Creating ways to be happy is your life's work, a challenge that won't end until you die. We'll come back to that in a minute. For now, the goal is just to try believing, or merely hoping, that even if all your loved ones remain toxically insane forever, it's still possible you'll find opportunities to thrive and joys to embrace.

### 4. Shift Your Focus from Controlling Your Loved One's Behavior to Creating Your Own Happiness

When I make this suggestion to my clients, they tend to take umbrage. "I always focus on creating my own happiness!" they insist. "That's precisely why I'm trying to get my grandchildren to visit, and my cat to stop biting, and Justin Bieber to engage with me in a mutually rewarding exchange of personal e-mails!"

Best of luck with that. Because as AA or any other 12-step group will tell you, sanity begins the moment you admit you're powerless over other people. This is the moment you become mentally free to start trying new ideas, building new relationships, experimenting to see what situations feel better than the hopeless deadlock of depending on change from someone you can't control.

Again, this is a lifelong project, a game of "You're getting warmer; you're getting colder" that stops only when you do. But the focus shift that helps you stop caring is like a little dance (drop hope of changing significant other, embrace determination to find alternative sources of peace and joy, step-ball-change) that immediately, reliably diverts your energy toward happiness and unconditional love.

## The Payoff

Once we'd established that I didn't care what happened to Loretta, our work together finally became productive. In a follow-up family session, I had each relative tell all the others, "I love you unconditionally—I don't care what happens to you." We discussed ways in which each of them might begin creating personal happiness, regardless of Loretta's actions. And as the focus shifted off her, Loretta felt less pressured, less harried, more respected. Smiles and hugs appeared in place of tension and tears.

Supported by her loving, uncaring family, Loretta eventually triumphed: She left Rex, got a job, and found a healthier mate. As you support your significant others, they may realize this same spectacular success. Or not. You can be happy either way, so what do you care? You have the freedom to live and let live, to love and let love. Granting yourself that freedom is one of the healthiest, most constructive things you can do for yourself and the people who matter to you. And if you disagree, I truly, respectfully, lovingly do not care.

JULY 2011

26096396R00123